Atlanta Braves 2020

A Baseball Companion

Edited by R.J. Anderson, Craig Goldstein and Bret Sayre

Baseball Prospectus

Craig Brown, Steven Goldman and David Pease, Consultant Editors
Robert Au, Harry Pavlidis and Amy Pircher, Statistics Editors

Copyright © 2020 by DIY Baseball, LLC.
All rights reserved

This book or any part thereof may not be reproduced or transmitted in any form or by any means, electronic or mechanical, including photocopying, recording, or by any information storage and retrieval system, without permission in writing from the publisher.

Limit of Liability/Disclaimer of Warranty: While the publisher and the author have used their best efforts in preparing this book, they make no representations or warranties with respect to the accuracy or completeness of the contents of this book and specifically disclaim any implied warranties of merchantability or fitness for a particular purpose. No warranty may be created or extended by sales representatives or written sales materials. The advice and strategies contained herein may not be suitable for your situation. You should consult with a professional where appropriate. Neither the publisher nor the author shall be liable for any loss of profit or any other commercial damages, including but not limited to special, incidental, consequential, or other damages.

Library of Congress Cataloging-in-Publication Data:
paperback
ISBN-13: 978-1-949332-96-4

Project Credits
Cover Design: Michael Byzewski at Aesthetic Apparatus
Interior Design and Production: Jeff Pease, Dave Pease
Layout: Jeff Pease, Dave Pease

Baseball icon courtesy of Uberux, from https://www.shareicon.net/author/uberux

Ballpark diagram courtesy of Lou Spirito/THIRTY81 Project, https://thirty81project.com/

Manufactured in the United States of America
10 9 8 7 6 5 4 3 2 1

Table of Contents

Statistical Introduction v

Part 1: Team Analysis

Atlanta Braves: Where Are You Going, Where Have You Been? 3
    Randy Holt, David Lee and Matthew Trueblood

Performance Graphs 7

2019 Team Performance 8

2020 Team Projections 9

Team Personnel 10

SunTrust Park Stats 11

Braves Team Analysis 13

Part 2: Player Analysis

Braves Player Analysis 18

Braves Prospects 99

Part 3: Featured Articles

The Baseball Is Juiced (Again) 117
    Robert Arthur

The Moral Hazard of Playing It Safe 121
    Craig Goldstein

Index of Names 127

Statistical Introduction

Sports are, fundamentally, a blend of athletic endeavor and storytelling. Baseball, like any other sport, tells its stories in so many ways: in the arc of a game from the stands or a season from the box scores, in photos, or even in numbers. At Baseball Prospectus, we understand that statistics don't replace observation or any of baseball's stories, but complement everything else that makes the game so much fun.

What stats help us with is with patterns and precision, variance and value. This book can help you learn things you may not see from watching a game or hundred, whether it's the path of a career over time or the breadth of the entire MLB. We'd also never ask you to choose between our numbers and the experience of viewing a game from the cheap seats or the comfort of your home; our publication combines running the numbers with observations and wisdom from some of the brightest minds we can find. But if you *do* want to learn more about the numbers beyond what's on the backs of player jerseys, let us help explain.

Offense

We've revised our methodology for determining batting value. Long-time readers of the book will notice that we've retired True Average in favor of a new metric: Deserved Runs Created Plus (DRC+). Developed by Jonathan Judge and our stats team, this statistic measures everything a player does at the plate–reaching base, hitting for power, making outs, and moving runners over–and puts it on a scale where 100 equals league-average performance. A DRC+ of 150 is terrific, a DRC+ of 100 is average and a DRC+ of 75 means you better be an excellent defender.

DRC+ also does a better job than any of our previous metrics in taking contextual factors into account. The model adjusts for how the park affects performance, but also for things like the talent of the opposing pitcher, value of different types of batted-ball events, league, temperature and other factors. It's able to describe a player's expected offensive contribution than any other statistic we've found over the years, and also does a better job of predicting future performance as well.

There's a lot more to DRC+'s story, and you can read all about it in greater depth near the end of this book.

The other aspect of run-scoring is baserunning, which we quantify using Baserunning Runs. BRR not only records the value of stolen bases (or getting caught in the act), but also accounts for all the stuff that doesn't show up on the back of a baseball card: a runner's ability to go first to third on a single, or advance on a fly ball.

Defense

Where offensive value is *relatively* easy to identify and understand, defensive value is…not. Over the past dozen years, the sabermetric community has focused mostly on stats based on zone data: a real-live human person records the type of batted ball and estimated landing location, and models are created that give expected outs. From there, you can compare fielders' actual outs to those expected ones. Simple, right?

Unfortunately, zone data has two major issues. First, zone data is recorded by commercial data providers who keep the raw data private unless you pay for it. (All the statistics we build in this book and on our website use public data as inputs.) That hurts our ability to test assumptions or duplicate results. Second, over the years it has become apparent that there's quite a bit of "noise" in zone-based fielding analysis. Sometimes the conclusions drawn from zone data don't hold up to scrutiny, and sometimes the different data provided by different providers don't look anything alike, giving wildly different results. Sometimes the hard-working professional stringers or scorers might unknowingly inflict unconscious bias into the mix: for example good fielders will often be credited with more expected outs despite the data, and ballparks with high press boxes tend to score more line drives than ones with a lower press box.

Enter our Fielding Runs Above Average (FRAA). For most positions, FRAA is built from play-by-play data, which allows us to avoid the subjectivity found in many other fielding metrics. The idea is this: count how many fielding plays are made by a given player and compare that to expected plays for an average fielder at their position (based on pitcher ground ball tendencies and batter handedness). Then we adjust for park and base-out situations.

When it comes to catchers, our methodology is a little different thanks to the laundry list of responsibilities they're tasked with beyond just, well, catching and throwing the ball. By now you've probably heard about "framing" or the art of making umpires more likely to call balls outside the strike zone for strikes. To put this into one tidy number, we incorporate pitch tracking data (for the years it exists) and adjust for important factors like pitcher, umpire, batter and home-field advantage using a mixed-model approach. This grants us a number for how many strikes the catcher is personally adding to (or subtracting from) his pitchers' performance…which we then convert to runs added or lost using linear weights.

Framing is one of the biggest parts of determining catcher value, but we also take into account blocking balls from going past, whether a scorer deems it a passed ball or a wild pitch. We use a similar approach—one that really benefits from the pitch tracking data that tells us what ends up in the dirt and what doesn't. We also include a catcher's ability to prevent stolen bases and how well they field balls in play, and *finally* we come up with our FRAA for catchers.

Pitching

Both pitching and fielding make up the half of baseball that isn't run scoring: run prevention. Separating pitching from fielding is a tough task, and most recent pitching analysis has branched off from Voros McCracken's famous (and controversial) statement, "There is little if any difference among major-league pitchers in their ability to prevent hits on balls hit in the field of play." The research of the analytic community has validated this to some extent, and there are a host of "defense-independent" pitching measures that have been developed to try and extract the effect of the defense behind a hurler from the pitcher's work.

Our solution to this quandary is Deserved Run Average (DRA), our core pitching metric. DRA looks like earned run average (ERA), the tried-and-true pitching stat you've seen on every baseball broadcast or box score from the past century, but it's very different. To start, DRA takes an event-by-event look at what the pitchers does, and adjusts the value of that event based on different environmental factors like park, batter, catcher, umpire, base-out situation, run differential, inning, defense, home field advantage, pitcher role and temperature. That mixed model gives us a pitcher's expected contribution, similar to what we do for our DRC+ model for hitters and FRAA model for catchers. (Oh, and we also consider the pitcher's effect on basestealing and on balls getting past the catcher.)

It's important to note that DRA is set to the scale of runs allowed per nine innings (RA9) instead of ERA, which makes DRA's scale slightly higher than ERA's. The reason for this is because ERA tends to overrate three types of pitchers:

1. Pitchers who play in parks where scorers hand out more errors. Official scorers differ significantly in the frequency at which they assign errors to fielders.
2. Ground-ball pitchers, because a substantial proportion of errors occur on groundballs.
3. Pitchers who aren't very good. Better pitchers often allow fewer unearned runs than bad pitchers, because good pitchers tend to find ways to get out of jams.

Since the last time you picked up an edition of this book, we've also made a few minor changes to DRA to make it better. Recent research into "tunneling"—the act of throwing consecutive pitches that appear similar from a batter's point of view until after the swing decision point–data has given us a new contextual factor to account for in DRA: plate distance. This refers to the distance between successive pitches as they approach the plate, and while it has a smaller effect than factors like velocity or whiff rate, it still can help explain pitcher strikeout rate in our model.

New Pitching Metrics for 2020

We're including a few "new" pitching metrics in the book for the 2020 edition, though unlike last year, these numbers may be a little bit more familiar to those of you who have spent some time investigating baseball statistics.

Fastball Percentage

Our fastball percentage (FB%) statistic measures how frequently a pitcher throws a pitch classified as a "fastball," measured as a percentage of overall pitches thrown. We qualify three types of fastballs:

1. The traditional four-seam fastball;
2. The two-seam fastball or sinker;
3. "Hard cutters," which are pitches that have the movement profile of a cut fastball and are used as the pitcher's primary offering or in place of a more traditional fastball.

For example, a pitcher with a FB% of 67 throws any combination of these three pitches about two-thirds of the time.

Whiff Rate

Everybody loves a swing and a miss, and whiff rate (WHF) measures how frequently pitchers induce a swinging strike. To calculate WHF, we add up all the pitches thrown that ended with a swinging strike, then divide that number by a pitcher's total pitches thrown. Most often, high whiff rates correlate with high strikeout rates (and overall effective pitcher performance).

Called Strike Probability

Called Strike Probability (CSP) is a number that represents the likelihood that all of a pitcher's pitches will be called a strike while controlling for location, pitcher and batter handedness, umpire and count. Here's how it works: on each pitch, our model determines how many times (out of 100) that a similar pitch was called for a strike given those factors mentioned above, and when normalized for each batter's strike zone. Then we average the CSP for all pitches thrown by a pitcher in a season, and that gives us the yearly CSP percentage you see in the stats boxes.

As you might imagine, pitchers with a higher CSP are more likely to work in the zone, where pitchers with a lower CSP are likely locating their pitches outside the normal strike zone, for better or for worse.

Projections

Many of you aren't turning to this book just for a look at what a player has done, but for a look at what a player is going to do: the PECOTA projections. PECOTA, initially developed by Nate Silver (who has moved on to greater fame as a political analyst), consists of three parts:

1. Major-league equivalencies, which use minor-league statistics to project how a player will perform in the major leagues;
2. Baseline forecasts, which use weighted averages and regression to the mean to estimate a player's current true talent level; and
3. Aging curves, which uses the career paths of comparable players to estimate how a player's statistics are likely to change over time.

With all those important things covered, let's take a look at what's in the book this year.

Team Prospectus

Most of this book is composed of team chapters, with one for each of the 30 major-league franchises. On the first page of each chapter, you'll see a box that contains some of the key statistics for each team as well as a very inviting stadium diagram. (You can see an example of this for the Milwaukee Brewers on this very page!)

We start with the team name, their unadjusted 2019 win-loss record, and their divisional ranking. Beneath that are a host of other team statistics. **Pythag** presents an adjusted 2019 winning percentage, calculated by taking runs scored per game (**RS/G**) and runs allowed per game (**RA/G**) for the team, and running them through a version of Bill James' Pythagorean formula that was refined and improved by David Smyth and Brandon Heipp. (The formula is called "Pythagenpat," which is equally fun to type and to say.)

Next up is **DRC+**, described earlier, to indicate the overall hitting ability of the team either above or below league-average. Run prevention on the pitching side is covered by **DRA** (also mentioned earlier) and another metric: Fielding Independent Pitching (**FIP**), which calculates another ERA-like statistic based on strikeouts, walks, and home runs recorded. Defensive Efficiency Rating (**DER**) tells us the percentage of balls in play turned into outs for the team, and is a quick fielding shorthand that rounds out run prevention.

After that, we have several measures related to roster composition, as opposed to on-field performance. **B-Age** and **P-Age** tell us the average age of a team's batters and pitchers, respectively. **Salary** is the combined team payroll for all on-field players, and Doug Pappas' Marginal Dollars per Marginal Win (**M$/MW**) tells us how much money a team spent to earn production above replacement level.

Ending this batch of statistics is the number of disabled list days a team had over the season (**IL Days**) and the amount of salary paid to players on the disabled list (**$ on IL**); this final number is expressed as a percentage of total payroll.

Next to each of these stats, we've listed each team's MLB rank in that category from first to 30th. In this, first always indicates a positive outcome and 30th a negative outcome, except in the case of salary—first is highest.

After the franchise statistics, we share a few items about the team's home ballpark. There's the aforementioned diagram of the park's dimensions (including distances to the outfield wall), a graphic showing the height of the wall from the left-field pole to the right-field pole, and a table showing three-year park factors for the stadium. The park factors are displayed as indexes where 100 is average, 110 means that the park inflates the statistic in question by 10 percent, and 90 means that the park deflates the statistic in question by 10 percent.

On the second page of each team chapter, you'll find three graphs. The first is the **2019 Hit List Ranking**. This shows our Hit List Rank for the team on each day of the 2019 season and is intended to give you a picture of the ups and downs of the team's season. Hit List Rank measures overall team performance and drives the Hit List Power Rankings at the baseballprospectus.com website.

The second graph is **Committed Payroll** and helps you see how the team's payroll has compared to the MLB and divisional average payrolls over time. Payroll figures are current as of January 1, 2020; with so many free agents still unsigned as of this writing, the final 2020 figure will likely be significantly different for many teams. (In the meantime, you can always find the most current data at Baseball Prospectus' Cot's Baseball Contracts page.)

The third graph is **Farm System Ranking** and displays how the Baseball Prospectus prospect team has ranked the organization's farm system since 2007.

After the graphs, we have a **Personnel** section that lists many of the important decision-makers and upper-level field and operations staff members for the franchise, as well as any former Baseball Prospectus staff members who are currently part of the organization. (In very rare circumstances, someone might be on both lists!)

Juan Soto LF
Born: 10/25/98   Age: 21   Bats: L   Throws: L
Height: 6'1"   Weight: 185   Origin: International Free Agent, 2015

YEAR	TEAM	LVL	AGE	PA	R	2B	3B	HR	RBI	BB	K	SB	CS	AVG/OBP/SLG
2017	NAT	RK	18	27	3	1	1	0	4	2	1	0	0	.320/.370/.440
2017	HAG	A	18	96	15	5	0	3	14	10	8	1	2	.360/.427/.523
2018	HAG	A	19	74	12	5	3	5	24	14	13	2	0	.373/.486/.814
2018	POT	A+	19	73	17	3	1	7	18	11	8	0	1	.371/.466/.790
2018	HAR	AA	19	35	4	2	0	2	10	4	7	1	0	.323/.400/.581
2018	WAS	MLB	19	494	77	25	1	22	70	79	99	5	2	.292/.406/.517
2019	WAS	MLB	20	659	110	32	5	34	110	108	132	12	1	.282/.401/.548
2020	WAS	MLB	21	630	92	30	3	35	102	85	123	5	2	.284/.382/.543

Comparables: Ronald Acuña Jr., Mike Trout, Tony Conigliaro

YEAR	TEAM	LVL	AGE	PA	DRC+	VORP	BABIP	BRR	FRAA	WARP
2017	NAT	RK	18	27	135	1.5	.333	0.0	RF(9): -1.1	0.0
2017	HAG	A	18	96	181	8.0	.373	1.0	RF(19): -1.9, LF(2): -0.3	0.9
2018	HAG	A	19	74	222	14.5	.405	0.3	RF(14): 1.1, CF(2): 0.2	1.2
2018	POT	A+	19	73	260	15.4	.340	1.4	RF(14): 1.0, LF(1): 0.0	1.6
2018	HAR	AA	19	35	113	3.6	.364	0.0	LF(4): 0.6, RF(4): -0.5	0.1
2018	WAS	MLB	19	494	125	40.5	.338	-0.5	LF(114): 2.7	3.0
2019	WAS	MLB	20	659	136	49.0	.312	1.4	LF(150): -0.8	4.9
2020	WAS	MLB	21	630	133	43.6	.310	-0.1	LF 3	4.8

Position Players

After all that information and a thoughtful bylined essay covering each team, we present our player comments. These are also bylined, but due to frequent franchise shifts during the offseason, our bylines are more a rough guide than a perfect accounting of who wrote what.

Each player is listed with the major-league team that employed him as of early January 2020. If a player changed teams after that point via free agency, trade, or any other method, you'll be able to find them in the chapter for their previous squad.

As an example, take a look at the player comment for Nationals outfielder Juan Soto: the stat block that accompanies his written comment is at the top of this page. First we cover biographical information (age is as of June 30, 2020) before moving onto the stats themselves. Our statistic columns include standard identifying information like **YEAR**, **TEAM**, **LVL** (level of affiliated play) and **AGE** before getting into the numbers. Next, we provide raw, untranslated numbers like you might find on the back of your dad's baseball cards: **PA** (plate appearances), **R** (runs), **2B** (doubles), **3B** (triples), **HR** (home runs), **RBI** (runs batted in), **BB** (walks), **K** (strikeouts), **SB** (stolen bases) and **CS** (caught stealing).

Statistical Introduction - xi

Next, we have unadjusted "slash" statistics: **AVG** (batting average), **OBP** (on-base percentage) and **SLG** (slugging percentage). Following the slash line is **DRC+** (Deserved Runs Created Plus), which we described earlier as total offensive expected contribution compared to the league average.

One of our oldest active metrics, **VORP** (Value Over Replacement Player), considers offensive production, position and plate appearances. In essence, it is the number of runs contributed beyond what a replacement-level player at the same position would contribute if given the same percentage of team plate appearances. VORP does not consider the quality of a player's defense.

BABIP (batting average on balls in play) tells us how often a ball in play fell for a hit, and can help us identify whether a batter may have been lucky or not...but note that high BABIPs also tend to follow the great hitters of our time, as well as speedy singles hitters who put the ball on the ground.

The next item is **BRR** (Baserunning Runs), which covers all of a player's baserunning accomplishments including (but not limited to) swiped bags and failed attempts. Next is **FRAA** (Fielding Runs Above Average), which also includes the number of games previously played at each position noted in parentheses. Multi-position players have only their two most frequent positions listed here, but their total FRAA number reflects all positions played.

Our last column here is **WARP** (Wins Above Replacement Player). WARP estimates the total value of a player, which means for hitters it takes into account hitting runs above average (calculated using the DRC+ model), BRR and FRAA. Then, it makes an adjustment for positions played and gives the player a credit for plate appearances based upon the difference between "replacement level"—which is derived from the quality of players added to a team's roster after the start of the season–and the league average.

The final line just below the stats box is **PECOTA** data, which is discussed further in a following section.

Catchers

Catchers are a special breed, and thus they have earned their own separate box which displays some of the defensive metrics that we've built just for them. As an example, let's check out J.T. Realmuto.

The **YEAR** and **TEAM** columns match what you'd find in the other stat box. **P. COUNT** indicates the number of pitches thrown while the catcher was behind the plate, including swinging strikes, fouls and balls in play. **FRM RUNS** is the total run value the catcher provided (or cost) his team by influencing the umpire to call strikes where other catchers did not. **BLK RUNS** expresses the total run value above or below average for the catcher's ability to prevent wild pitches and passed balls. **THRW RUNS** is calculated using a similar model as the previous two statistics, and it measures a catcher's ability to throw out basestealers but also to dissuade them from testing his arm in the first place. It takes into account factors like the pitcher (including his delivery and pickoff move) and baserunner (who could be as fast as Billy Hamilton or as slow as Yonder Alonso). **TOT RUNS** is the sum of all of the previous three statistics.

Justin Verlander   RHP
Born: 02/20/83   Age: 37   Bats: R   Throws: R
Height: 6'5"   Weight: 225   Origin: Round 1, 2004 Draft (#2 overall)

YEAR	TEAM	LVL	AGE	W	L	SV	G	GS	IP	H	HR	BB/9	K/9	K	GB%	BABIP
2017	DET	MLB	34	10	8	0	28	28	172	153	23	3.5	9.2	176	34%	.283
2017	HOU	MLB	34	5	0	0	5	5	34	17	4	1.3	11.4	43	32%	.194
2018	HOU	MLB	35	16	9	0	34	34	214	156	28	1.6	12.2	290	31%	.272
2019	HOU	MLB	36	21	6	0	34	34	223	137	36	1.7	12.1	300	36%	.219
2020	HOU	MLB	37	15	6	0	29	29	184	138	28	2.3	12.1	248	35%	.274

Comparables: Zack Greinke, A.J. Burnett, Aníbal Sánchez

YEAR	TEAM	LVL	AGE	WHIP	ERA	DRA	WARP	MPH	FB%	WHF	CSP
2017	DET	MLB	34	1.28	3.82	4.03	3.0	97.7	58	11	47.8
2017	HOU	MLB	34	0.65	1.06	3.08	0.9	97.5	59.6	15.1	49.9
2018	HOU	MLB	35	0.90	2.52	2.33	7.3	97.5	61.2	16.2	51.6
2019	HOU	MLB	36	0.80	2.58	2.51	7.9	96.8	49.9	17.5	48.3
2020	HOU	MLB	37	1.01	2.75	2.95	5.3	95.8	54.6	15.1	48.2

Pitchers

Let's give our pitchers a turn, using 2019 AL Cy Young winner Justin Verlander as our example. Take a look at his stat block: the first line and the **YEAR**, **TEAM**, **LVL** and **AGE** columns are the same as in the position player example earlier.

Here too, we have a series of columns that display raw, unadjusted statistics compiled by the pitcher over the course of a season: **W** (wins), **L** (losses), **SV** (saves), **G** (games pitched), **GS** (games started), **IP** (innings pitched), **H** (hits allowed) and **HR** (home runs allowed). Next we have two statistics that are rates: **BB/9** (walks per nine innings) and **K/9** (strikeouts per nine innings), before returning to the unadjusted K (strikeouts).

Next up is **GB%** (ground ball percentage), which is the percentage of all batted balls that were hit on the ground, including both outs and hits. Remember, this is based on observational data and subject to human error, so please approach this with a healthy dose of skepticism.

BABIP (batting average on balls in play) is calculated using the same methodology as it is for position players, but it often tells us more about a pitcher than it does a hitter. With pitchers, a high BABIP is often due to poor defense or bad luck, and can often be an indicator of potential rebound, and a low BABIP may be cause to expect performance regression. (A typical league-average BABIP is close to .290-.300.)

The metrics **WHIP** (walks plus hits per inning pitched) and **ERA** (earned run average) are old standbys: WHIP measures walks and hits allowed on a per-inning basis, while ERA measures earned runs on a nine-inning basis. Neither of these stats are translated or adjusted.

DRA (Deserved Run Average) was described at length earlier, and measures how many runs the pitcher "deserved" to allow per nine innings. Please note that since we lack all the data points that would make for a "real" DRA for minor-league events, the DRA displayed for minor league partial-seasons is based off of different data. (That data is a modified version of our cFIP metric, which you can find more information about on our website.)

Just like with hitters, **WARP** (Wins Above Replacement Player) is a total value metric that puts pitchers of all stripes on the same scale as position players. We use DRA as the primary input for our calculation of WARP. You might notice that relief pitchers (due to their limited innings) may have a lower WARP than you were expecting or than you might see in other WARP-like metrics. WARP does not take leverage into account, just the actions a pitcher performs and the expected value of those actions...which ends up judging high-leverage relief pitchers differently than you might imagine given their prestige and market value.

MPH gives you the pitcher's 95th percentile velocity for the noted season, in order to give you an idea of what the *peak* fastball velocity a pitcher possesses. Since this comes from our pitch-tracking data, it is not publicly available for minor-league pitchers.

Finally, we display the three new pitching metrics we described earlier. **FB%** (fastball percentage) gives you the percentage of fastballs thrown out of all pitches. **WHF** (whiff rate) tells you the percentage of swinging strikes induced out of all pitches. **CSP** (called strike probability) expresses the likelihood of all pitches thrown to result in a called strike, after controlling for factors like handedness, umpire, pitch type, count and location.

PECOTA

All players have PECOTA projections for 2020, as well as a set of other numbers that describe the performance of comparable players according to PECOTA. All projections for 2020 are for the player at the date we went to press in early January and are projected into the league and park context as indicated by the team abbreviation. (Note that players at very low levels of the minors are too unpredictable to assess using these numbers.) All PECOTA projected statistics represent a player's projected major-league performance.

Below the projections are the player's three highest-scoring comparable players as determined by PECOTA. All comparables represent a snapshot of how the listed player was performing at the same age as the current player, so if a

23-year-old pitcher is compared to Bartolo Colón, he's actually being compared to a 23-year-old Colón, not the version that pitched for the Rangers in 2018, nor to Colón's career as a whole.

A few points about pitcher projections. First, we aren't yet projecting peak velocity, so that column will be blank in the PECOTA lines. Second, projecting DRA is trickier than evaluating past performance, because it is unclear how deserving each pitcher will be of his anticipated outcomes. However, we know that another DRA-related statistic–contextual FIP or cFIP-estimates future run scoring very well. So for PECOTA, the projected DRA figures you see are based on the past cFIPs generated by the pitcher and comparable players over time, along with the other factors described above.

Lineouts

In each chapter's Lineouts section, you'll find abbreviated text comments, as well as all the same information you'd find in our full player comments. The only difference is that we limit the stats boxes in this section to only including the 2019 information for each player.

Managers

After all those wonderful team chapters, we've got statistics for each big-league manager, all of whom are organized by alphabetical order. Here you'll find a block including an extraordinary amount of information collected from each manager's entire career. For more information on the acronyms and what they mean, please visit the Glossary at www.baseballprospectus.com.

There is one important metric that we'd like to call attention to, and you'll find it next to each manager's name: **wRM+** (weighted reliever management plus). Developed by Rob Arthur and Rian Watt, wRM+ investigates how good a manager is at using their best relievers during the moments of highest leverage, using both our proprietary DRA metric as well as Leverage Index. wRM+ is scaled to a league average of 100, and a wRM+ of 105 indicates that relievers were used approximately five percent "better" than average. On the other hand, a wRM+ of 95 would tell us the team used its relievers five percent "worse" than the average team.

While wRM+ does not have an extremely strong correlation with a manager, it is statistically significant; this means that a manager is not *entirely* responsible for a team's wRM+, but does have some effect on that number.

PECOTA Leaderboards

If you're familiar with PECOTA, then you'll have noticed that the projection system often appears bullish on players coming off a bad year and bearish on players coming off a good year. (This is because the system weights several previous seasons, not just the most recent one.) In addition, we publish the 50th

Atlanta Braves 2020

percentile projections for each player–which is smack in the middle of the range of projected production—which tends to mean PECOTA stat lines don't often have extreme results like 40 home runs or 250 strikeouts in a given season. In essence, PECOTA doesn't project very many extreme seasons.

At the end of the book, we've ranked the top players at each position based on their PECOTA projections. This might help you visualize just how a given player's projection compares to that of their peers, so that even if a dramatic stat line isn't projected, you can still imagine how they stack up against the rest of the league.

Part 1: Team Analysis

Atlanta Braves: Where Are You Going, Where Have You Been?

Randy Holt, David Lee and Matthew Trueblood

2019: What Went Right
With marquee additions in Philadelphia, a retooled Washington squad, and a Mets team that was supposed to be at least marginally better, many predicted the National League East to be a gauntlet the Braves would fail to run. An 85-77 preseason projection from PECOTA had Atlanta finishing behind all three. But the Braves proved those tempered expectations wrong, finishing with a 97-65 record, four games better than second-place Washington. Additionally, their +112 run differential ended up fourth-best in the National League.

Perhaps the most notable element (and most essential given its impact on the future) was the way the offense came together. The Braves dealt with numerous health-related challenges to their depth, but the core group largely remained healthy and productive throughout the season. Ronald Acuña Jr, Atlanta's franchise player, built on a strong rookie campaign. He nearly had the first 40/40 season in Braves history. A late-season injury held him at 37 steals, but he finished with a slash of .280/.365/.518 and that'll do. His ISO, while a bit of a drop from 2018, still came in at .238, thanks to the 22 doubles and 41 homers. Overall, he finished with a 6.1 WARP due to the combination of offensive and defensive prowess (2.7 FRAA). He looked tired at times late in the year, and then there was the groin injury at the end of September, but there isn't any doubt about his place among the game's elite outfielders.

The Braves demonstrated in 2019 that they can have as deep and productive a lineup as anybody in the National League. Ozzie Albies had a career year in nearly every regard. Freddie Freeman faded down the stretch, but overall had a characteristically good season. Josh Donaldson was every bit the one-year free agent steal he was projected to be, reaching base at a near-.380 clip and slugging .521. With still-developing talents like Austin Riley and Dansby Swanson showing flashes of offensive competence (Riley early in the year, Swanson in the postseason), this lineup proved it can be dangerous for years to come.

While the club didn't boast an overwhelmingly impressive pitching staff as a whole, Mike Soroka was the breakout star of the rotation. Given his prior shoulder woes, concerns over Soroka's immediate and long-term future were justified, but he made 29 starts, posting a 2.68 ERA and a 3.24 DRA for the year, striking out 7.3 per nine and walking 2.1. His groundball rate was up over 50 percent as well. He also demonstrated slight decreases in barrels allowed and average exit velocity. In the Year of the Juiced Ball, that's probably worth noting. He did virtually everything you could have asked of a young potential frontline starter.

Only two National League teams scored more runs than the Braves, and only three hit more home runs. In a league where steals have faded, they ranked fourth in the NL. And, for those who value oddly-specific-but-super-important-statistics: Nobody scored more runs in the seventh inning or later than the Braves. They failed disastrously in Games 4 & 5 of the NLDS, but in general they showed a resilience that most clubs would covet.

2019: What Went Wrong

It's not as if the Atlanta Braves were a tremendously flawed franchise that masked glaring shortcomings in their roster construction with long balls (See: Cubs, Chicago). The Braves didn't have systematic issues that contributed to their ultimate demise, ugly as the end may have been. Instead, it was just a matter of coming up short in a few key areas. Those two areas were predominantly pitching and physical health.

The pitching staff was mostly middle-of-the-road. The Braves had a staff ERA of 4.19, but ranked in the bottom half of the Senior Circuit in strikeouts, whiff rate, and WHIP, while also sporting the fifth-highest walk rate and seventh-highest hard contact rate in the NL. It's not as if the pitching staff was a flaming disaster night-in and night-out. They were just average. Their young arms had difficulty demonstrating consistency and some had to adjust to multiple roles in and out of the bullpen.

From a health perspective, the Braves had 21 players hit the injured list at some point during the season, according to Spotrac. That was the seventh-most in all of baseball. Again, they didn't lose games to injury in the way that say, the Yankees did, but they lost depth. This became a massive issue once the postseason rolled around. Pitching and depth are essential ingredients to a championship roster, and the Braves clearly suffered at the tail end of the season because of a lack of both.

Then there's the defense. Atlanta ranked 22nd in the league in defensive efficiency despite a pitching staff that served up a 46.5 percent groundball rate, third highest in the league. Logic says those ground balls should have translated into more outs, but that wasn't the case. The Braves had six players start more than 100 games in 2019. Three of those players were below average according to FRAA: Albies, Freeman, and aging outfielder Nick Markakis. Similar to the pitching staff, this wasn't a terminal flaw, but shoring up the defense will definitely be a necessity, both in the starting lineup and on the bench.

The Braves lost a winner-take-all playoff game in about the most deflating way possible, but this was a 97-win team and (relatively) convincing champion in arguably the deepest division in baseball. Yet another early playoff exit given that regular season success is tough to swallow, and the Braves will enter 2020 with a core still in place (minus Donaldson), but also still looking to get over the hump. —*Randy Holt*

Prospect Outlook

The Braves are a model organization when it comes to using homegrown pieces to their advantage. They're currently enjoying an infusion of prospect talent that has arrived in two waves. The first produced the likes of Acuña Jr., Albies, Soroka, and Max Fried. The second wave should start to impact the big-league team in 2020. **Cristian Pache**, **Drew Waters**, and **Ian Anderson** should begin carving out their roles by the end of the 2020 season. They're the consensus top three players in the system. Pache and Waters should eventually vie for the remaining spot beside Acuña and Marcell Ozuna (Ozuna is on a one-year contract, so the blockage may be temporary), with Anderson shouldering his way into a rotation spot. Behind them, **Kyle Wright** still has at least mid-rotation stuff if he can get over the mental hump of pitching in the majors, and **Bryse Wilson** can provide a multi-innings boost to the bullpen or as a back-end starter. Don't sleep on **Kyle Muller** as a solid left-handed power arm that should contribute soon.

Get past that talented half-dozen and the system begins to thin quickly. The Braves tried to address lower-level depth concerns with late-round athletes this past draft, but it's going to be a serious struggle to maintain the system's lofty status going forward. That's much easier to swallow when you have one of the youngest and most talented major-league teams in the game. —*David Lee*

2020 Outlook

Alex Anthopoulos got himself into trouble in 2018 (well, what passes for trouble these days, anyway; Twitter complained about him) by talking about financial flexibility as though it were an end unto itself. It isn't, and shouldn't be, and Anthopoulos knows that. Yet, he works for a corporate ownership group that doesn't offer him especially wide discretion in terms of spending, so maintaining the team's agility does matter, even if building a great roster matters more.

Given that premise, Anthopoulos had perhaps the best offseason he could have had. He used the money coming off the team's books after 2019 and the uncertainty of the early days of free agency to snap up Will Smith and Chris

Martin on very affordable deals. Smith, Martin, Greene, and Melancon form a veteran bullpen quartet with an impeccable recent track record, and it didn't cost the team a prohibitive sum to assemble it.

Smith signed with Atlanta rather than accept the qualifying offer from the Giants, so the Braves did lose a future draft pick in the process. However, the financial terms of the deal not only make that tradeoff palatable for the Braves in the short term but remove any pressure the team might have felt to commit to Melancon or Greene beyond 2020. The biggest weakness of last year's Braves will be a strength this time around.

Nor was Smith the only case in which it seemed as though Anthopoulos read the market perfectly and used that knowledge to preserve his own flexibility and leverage. Cole Hamels signed for $18 million, but on just a one-year deal. Nearly two months later, Ozuna signed on the same terms. In the meantime, of course, the team lost Donaldson to the Twins, but the difference between Donaldson's ultimate price tag and Ozuna's makes the value calculus performed by Anthopoulos impossible to ignore. In the tradeoff of Donaldson for Ozuna, the Braves get back a draft pick, and they also get to wait a year before pressing Pache or Waters into full-time service in the outfield, a delaying tactic also aided by re-upping Markakis for one more year. Then again, if either proves they're ready, the path remains clear for them.

Travis d'Arnaud signed a two-year deal that seems to position him as a sturdy stopgap while the team waits to see whether either William Contreras or Shea Langoliers can quickly assert themselves to be ready. One by one, moves like these have piled up. Before being shoved aside in Toronto by a different corporate owner in favor of a more ruthlessly value-focused executive, Anthopoulos frequently showed a flair for threading the needle, finding impact additions to good teams even while remaining focused on flexibility and sustainability. Thus far, his Braves tenure has been an affirmation of that talent, and a rebuke of the Blue Jays' hyperopic choice years ago. Anthopoulos didn't assemble all the young talent now making Atlanta a budding powerhouse, but he's overseen its coalescence and kept it from going to waste. —*Matthew Trueblood*

Performance Graphs

2019 Hit List Ranking

Committed Payroll (in millions)

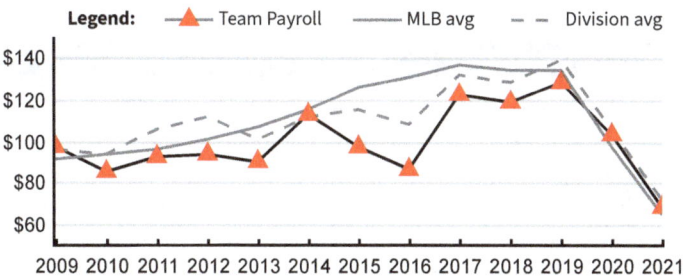

Farm System Ranking

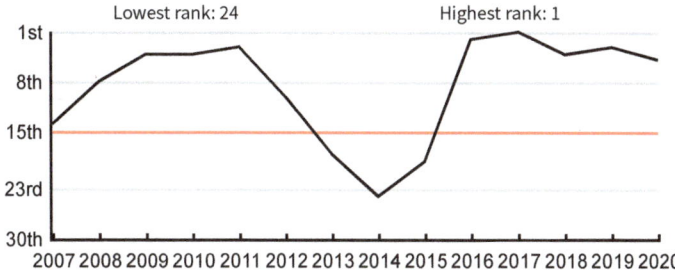

2019 Team Performance

ACTUAL STANDINGS

Team	W	L	Pct
ATL	**97**	**65**	**0.599**
WAS	93	69	0.574
NYN	86	76	0.531
PHI	81	81	0.500
MIA	57	105	0.352

THIRD-ORDER STANDINGS

Team	W	L	Pct
WAS	95	67	0.584
ATL	**89**	**73**	**0.550**
NYN	88	74	0.542
PHI	74	88	0.457
MIA	60	102	0.373

TOP HITTERS

Player	WARP
Ronald Acuña Jr.	6.1
Josh Donaldson	5.1
Ozzie Albies	4.4

TOP PITCHERS

Player	WARP
Mike Soroka	4.8
Max Fried	4.2
Julio Teheran	2.2

VITAL STATISTICS

Statistic Name	Value	Rank
Pythagenpat	.567	9th
Runs Scored per Game	5.28	7th
Runs Allowed per Game	4.59	12th
Deserved Runs Created Plus	104	7th
Deserved Run Average	4.39	10th
Fielding Independent Pitching	4.34	13th
Defensive Efficiency Rating	.698	21st
Batter Age	27.9	19th
Pitcher Age	27.1	5th
Salary	$128.2M	14th
Marginal $ per Marginal Win	$2.4M	27th
Injured List Days	947	9th
$ on IL	16%	18th

2020 Team Projections

PROJECTED STANDINGS

Team	W	L	Pct	+/-
NYN	87.8	74.2	0.542	2
WAS	87.1	74.9	0.538	-6
ATL	**82.8**	**79.2**	**0.511**	**-14**
PHI	76.8	85.2	0.474	-4
MIA	71.3	90.7	0.440	14

TOP PROJECTED HITTERS

Player	WARP
Freddie Freeman	4.0
Ronald Acuña Jr.	4.0
Ozzie Albies	3.1

TOP PROJECTED PITCHERS

Player	WARP
Mike Soroka	2.4
Mike Foltynewicz	1.9
Max Fried	1.6

FARM SYSTEM REPORT

Top Prospect	Number of Top 101 Prospects
Cristian Pache, #22	6

KEY DEDUCTIONS

Player	WARP
Josh Donaldson	3.0
Dallas Keuchel	1.6
Julio Teheran	1.2
Matt Joyce	0.6
Francisco Cervelli	0.6
John Ryan Murphy	0.1
Anthony Swarzak	0.0

KEY ADDITIONS

Player	WARP
Travis d'Arnaud	2.0
Marcell Ozuna	1.9
Will Smith	1.3
Cole Hamels	1.1
Ian Anderson	0.7
Cristian Pache	0.3
Drew Waters	0.2
Kyle Muller	0.1
Tucker Davidson	0.1
Yonder Alonso	0.0

Team Personnel

Executive Vice President, General Manager
Alex Anthopoulos

Vice President, Baseball Operations & Assistant General Manager
Perry Minasian

Assistant General Manager, Research and Development
Jason Paré

Assistant General Manager, Major League Operations
Alex Tamin

Special Assistant to the General Manager
Mike Fast

Manager
Brian Snitker

BP Alumni
Mike Fast
Jason Paré
Ronit Shah
Noah Woodward
Smith Brickner
Colin Wyers

SunTrust Park Stats

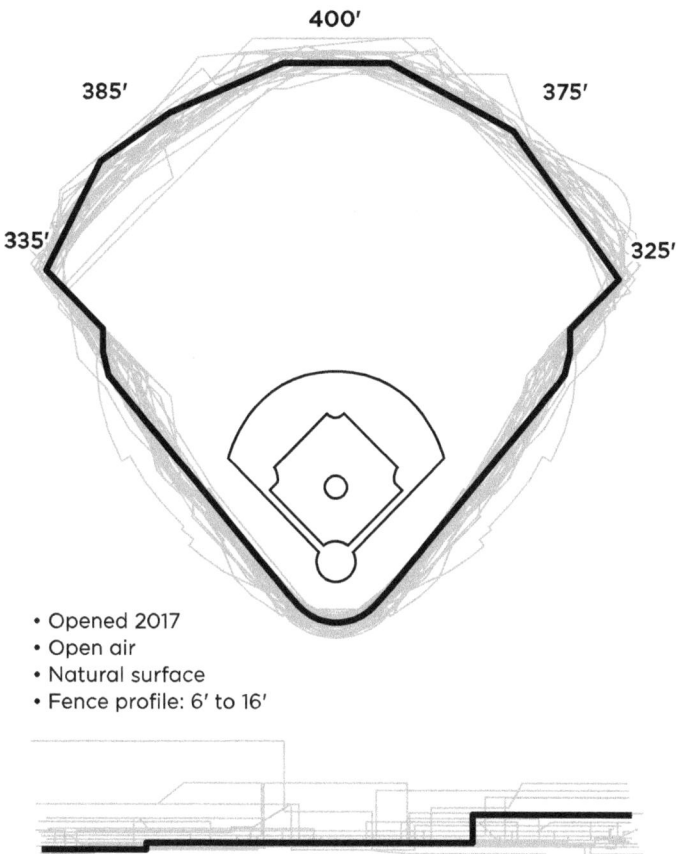

- Opened 2017
- Open air
- Natural surface
- Fence profile: 6' to 16'

Three-Year Park Factors

Runs	Runs/RH	Runs/LH	HR/RH	HR/LH
102	101	105	94	100

Braves Team Analysis

Trying to sum up a season with a play is daffy. It requires swapping out nuance and accuracy for narrative tidiness, giving into the convenient logic of turning points and crucial moments. In baseball—162 games, some 300 pitches in each of them, countless veers of defense and decision-making and baserunning—the impulse is even more ridiculous. In no game is a player less reducible to a moment.

So—well, here goes.

The moment of Ronald Acuña, Jr.'s spectacular second season that sticks in my mind came in early May, during a game at Dodger Stadium. The Braves trailed 3-0 when Clayton Kershaw threw Acuña a lumpy curve, low but not low enough. Acuña waited on it, barreled it, held a one-handed—*that's f***ing right*—follow-through as it went backspinning over the right field wall. It was his seventh home run of the season, just the 33rd of his career.

The homer didn't end up much mattering; the Braves lost, 9-4. Nor was it all that stylistically distinct. Just eight months into his big-league career, Acuña was by last spring already known for his all-fields power and his ability to get to pitches in the depths of the strike zone. He had already hit six homers on the season, emerging as the most promising young player, production-wise and entertainment-value-wise, in the sport. He stole bases and laced doubles and cracked moonshots and let go of throws that sprouted rocket-boosters. He had all five tools and a baby face. He dropped his bat coolly and ran out from under his helmet even more coolly.

Still, there was something about the homer off Kershaw. Part of it, to be sure, was the generational aspect, the immortal-for-now kid versus the now-mortal legend. But the greater part was the basic visible makeup of the play. A hanging curve, especially one presented to a slugger in the heady environment of the late-2010s, is a chance to pull the ball, to get the swing started early and the hips involved heavily. But Acuña had waited on it. He'd held his hands back, kept his weight from spilling out over the plate, made hitting coaches swoon. *Then* he became the dynamo. The ball went over the opposite-field wall about as fast and hard as any baseball goes anywhere. It was an instance of fundamentals-as-performance, a kind of flashy citation. He did it because he could.

Acuña, of course, serves as the centerpiece for a resurgent Braves franchise stocked well with young power arms and position players, and seasoned tastefully with veteran presence. He's the best reason Atlanta fans have to hope for another stretch atop the NL East. To baseball at large, he's something more interesting: that player who comes along every now and again with the ability to do very nearly whatever he wants. He ended up hitting 41 homers last year, and he swiped 37 bases. He persistently nudged the daily possibilities of baseball a little outward. All-Star games await him as a matter of course; MVPs seem almost inevitable.

Fans have the unavoidable tendency, with a player like Acuña, to forecast. As he gets stronger and his swing gets even sharper, as he sees more pitches and hones his approach, potential will harden into consistency. He remains, for now and by the coldest calculations, a smidge overenthusiastic about the spectacular play and bored by the routine one. His production can tip toward the highlight. But if the Braves' realization of their goals rests in large part on Acuña's maturation, their supporters would do well to enjoy another year of the version they get to watch now. Growing up, in baseball as in everything else, means giving something of yourself away.

⚾ ⚾ ⚾

Last October, in Game 1 of the Division Series against the St. Louis Cardinals, Acuña put another lovely swing on another not-good-enough breaking ball, sending it more than 350 feet down the right field line. Acuña thought it was gone and broke into a home-run trot, but it pulled up short and bounced off the wall, and the lack of an out-of-the-box sprint kept him to a single.

The dreaded accusation—a lack of hustle—had landed on Acuña before, most notably following a similar play in a loss to the Dodgers in August. "The name on the front is a lot more important than the name on the back of that jersey," Atlanta manager Brian Snitker had said then, and Acuña had concurred: "There's no excuse for it." After the Cardinals capped their Game 1 NLDS win, despite a ninth-inning bomb from Acuña making things more interesting, the tsk-ing repeated. "It's kind of beating a dead horse after that if you keep having the same conversation over and over again," first baseman Freddie Freeman said after the game. "You have to know that was a mistake." "He probably scores in that inning if he's on second base," second baseman Ozzie Albies said. "It's a big deal. He knows he needs to do better there."

The Braves had a reasonable enough gripe, of course; you'd be hard-pressed to find anyone in professional baseball who would shrug at leaving runs on the table in the middle of the summer, much less October. Still, there was something arch and archetypal to the messaging, a shared lineage with evil headmasters and draconian wardens. As the Braves went on to lose the series in five games, Acuña was a rare bright spot; the 21-year-old tallied eight hits, five of them going for extra bases, for a 1.454 OPS. He had made a young player's mistake in Game 1, but he'd spent the rest of the series playing with a young player's fearlessness.

Hustle—like strike-zone discipline and solid baserunning and commitment to scouting-report preparation—is commonly understood to be a straightforward positive. It costs nothing but effort. What if this isn't the case? What if the youthful impulse that has Acuña occasionally lollygagging it out of the batter's box is the same one that lets him risk allowing a triple to dive for the ball in the gap? That lets him bring a slow pulse to the biggest games of the year? That lets him not only plaster a future Hall of Famer's signature pitch but decide exactly how he wants to plaster it, with what combination of approach and discipline and all-out style, to what part of the park?

⚾ ⚾ ⚾

It's more or less a sure thing that Acuña will improve in the aforementioned areas. The *Journal-Constitution* will run a story in March on his commitment to sprinting out every grounder. In May, people will be tracking a climbing OBP and a more reasonable strikeout-to-walk rate. Television announcers will take care to note his hitting the cutoff man. The data points and anecdotes will be presented as benchmarks along the trajectory linking phenom to franchise player. The word that will be invoked is "consistency," another of those uncomplicatedly good baseball values.

It's the way of things. Baseball seasons are long, and for good players, there are a lot of them. Habits build; they may as well be useful ones.

Soon enough, Acuña will be a constant. His statistical profile will have changed; there will be fewer steals (unneeded risk), more bases on balls (better pitch recognition), and lengthier plate appearances (improved discipline). His attention will shift toward the grind and away from the moment. The talk of a 40-40 season—the kind he might have had last year but for an injury that had him sitting the last week—will go away, but no matter. In all corners, he'll be a new-and-improved Ronald Acuña, Jr., a player whose promise is being cashed in. He'll sit in the middle of the Braves' lineup, and, if everyone else does their part, Atlanta will win a lot of games.

There's some sadness here. It's something like the sadness of a young pitcher dropping a dizzying but inconsistent breaking ball to hone his other pitches, or of a hitter succumbing to a career of platoon duties, or of Mike Trout, former all-everything wonder, stealing only 11 bases last season. There are no uncomplicated positives in baseball. They all come at the cost of something: immediacy, personality, hope, ideas of one's best self. They affirm that the reasons to play baseball and the ways of playing winning baseball are not always quite the same thing.

For now, Acuña still sits in that point in his career where things are not yet fully habitual. Even given his young age—what is it about reaching the big leagues that blots out all other context?—this is a source of some frustration to his fans and teammates. It is also the best reason to watch him. Soon enough, he'll run out all his grounders, and soon enough, when he gets a hanging breaking ball, he'll do just what all of the other great hitters around the game do: Pull it to left, drop his bat, and get around the bases.

—Robert O'Connell is a freelance sportswriter whose work has appeared in The Athletic and Deadspin.

Part 2: Player Analysis

Atlanta Braves 2020

PLAYER COMMENTS WITH GRAPHS

Ozzie Albies 2B
Born: 01/07/97   Age: 23   Bats: B   Throws: R
Height: 5'8"   Weight: 165   Origin: International Free Agent, 2013

YEAR	TEAM	LVL	AGE	PA	R	2B	3B	HR	RBI	BB	K	SB	CS	AVG/OBP/SLG
2017	GWN	AAA	20	448	67	21	8	9	41	28	90	21	2	.285/.330/.440
2017	ATL	MLB	20	244	34	9	5	6	28	21	36	8	1	.286/.354/.456
2018	ATL	MLB	21	684	105	40	5	24	72	36	116	14	3	.261/.305/.452
2019	ATL	MLB	22	702	102	43	8	24	86	54	112	15	4	.295/.352/.500
2020	ATL	MLB	23	595	66	33	6	19	74	40	98	17	5	.269/.324/.455

Comparables: Rougned Odor, Ted Lepcio, Carlos Correa

After hitting more homers in 2018 than he had in his entire pro career (majors and minors) to that point, the big question was whether Albies' power was here to stay. It turns out that the diminutive second baseman answered "yes" to a different question: Could he keep some of the power gains while showcasing the batting average and on-base skills he demonstrated in the minors? Albies still swings a lot—his 56 percent swing rate was eighth in the majors last season—but that's here to stay and it's a feature, not a bug. The next frontier for the Curacao native is not a small one: improving against right-handed pitching. For the second straight year, Albies showed a massive split and his overall numbers in 2019 were buoyed by a staggering .389/.414/.685 line against southpaws. Still just 23 for the entire 2020 season, there's plenty of time to continue providing answers for the things standing between Albies and stardom.

YEAR	TEAM	LVL	AGE	PA	DRC+	VORP	BABIP	BRR	FRAA	WARP
2017	GWN	AAA	20	448	109	27.2	.342	3.3	2B(82): 3.8, SS(14): -2.0	2.3
2017	ATL	MLB	20	244	109	14.2	.316	0.6	2B(57): -2.9	0.8
2018	ATL	MLB	21	684	106	33.1	.285	5.9	2B(157): 7.0	4.0
2019	ATL	MLB	22	702	119	41.3	.325	4.4	2B(158): -0.4	4.4
2020	ATL	MLB	23	595	101	27.8	.297	2.8	2B 2	3.0

Ozzie Albies, continued

Batted Ball Distribution

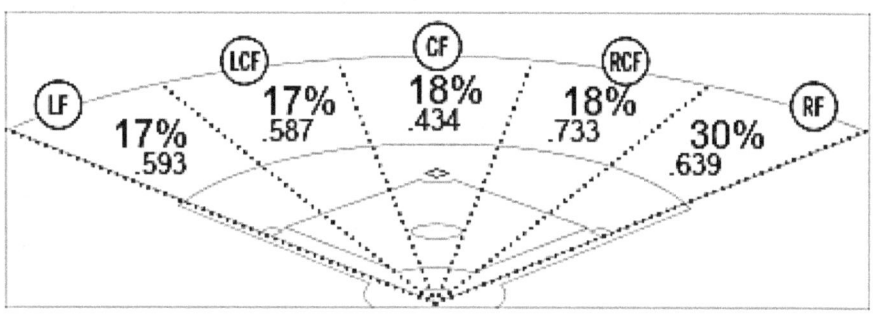

Strike Zone vs LHP   **Strike Zone vs RHP**

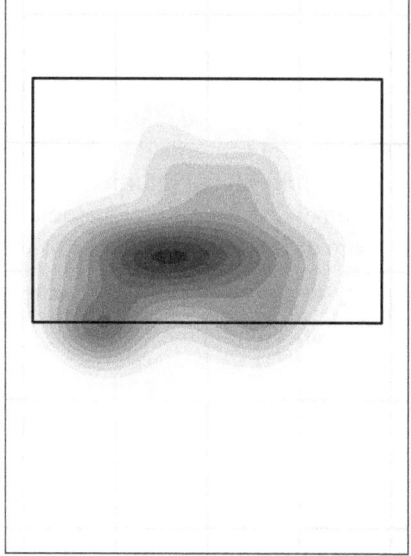

Atlanta Braves 2020

Johan Camargo UT
Born: 12/13/93 Age: 26 Bats: B Throws: R
Height: 6'0" Weight: 195 Origin: International Free Agent, 2010

YEAR	TEAM	LVL	AGE	PA	R	2B	3B	HR	RBI	BB	K	SB	CS	AVG/OBP/SLG
2017	GWN	AAA	23	142	17	9	1	4	20	8	22	1	0	.295/.340/.473
2017	ATL	MLB	23	256	30	21	2	4	27	12	51	0	0	.299/.331/.452
2018	GWN	AAA	24	36	6	2	0	3	7	3	9	0	0	.303/.361/.636
2018	ATL	MLB	24	524	63	27	1	19	76	51	108	1	1	.272/.349/.457
2019	GWN	AAA	25	64	10	6	0	2	15	5	12	0	0	.483/.531/.690
2019	ATL	MLB	25	248	31	12	1	7	32	15	43	1	0	.233/.279/.384
2020	ATL	MLB	26	399	41	21	2	12	47	25	76	1	0	.252/.303/.415

Comparables: Lonnie Chisenhall, Didi Gregorius, Cody Asche

During rebuilds, you always hear about prospects as it can be hard for fans to get it up for the players who are actively contributing to the poor major-league product. Much less attention is paid to the young players who weren't fawned over on prospect lists but still play their way into a role with that first-wave contender. Such was the case with Camargo, who rose out of anonymity and into the starting lineup with the Braves more out of necessity than anything else. The arrival of Josh Donaldson indeed pushed Camargo back to the fringes and he returned to the role of utilityman, playing every non-pitching position in 2019 except for centerfield and catcher. Unfortunately, as Camargo went back to a reduced role, his bat returned to its pre-2018 form. Still a force against lefties on a team without a natural platoon partner, Camargo will need to continue to evolve in order to keep a defined role on this now-contending team.

YEAR	TEAM	LVL	AGE	PA	DRC+	VORP	BABIP	BRR	FRAA	WARP
2017	GWN	AAA	23	142	112	8.6	.324	-0.2	SS(31): -6.4, 3B(2): 0.2	0.1
2017	ATL	MLB	23	256	86	16.1	.364	3.0	3B(43): -0.4, SS(26): 0.6	0.8
2018	GWN	AAA	24	36	134	3.5	.333	0.3	SS(4): -0.5, 3B(3): -0.2	0.2
2018	ATL	MLB	24	524	116	34.2	.315	-1.6	3B(114): -9.8, SS(18): -1.5	1.6
2019	GWN	AAA	25	64	186	11.1	.591	-1.9	3B(7): -0.6, SS(4): 0.3	0.6
2019	ATL	MLB	25	248	80	3.0	.258	0.2	SS(25): 0.5, 3B(18): -0.2	0.3
2020	ATL	MLB	26	399	86	4.8	.287	0.5	3B -3, 2B 0	0.1

Johan Camargo, continued

Batted Ball Distribution

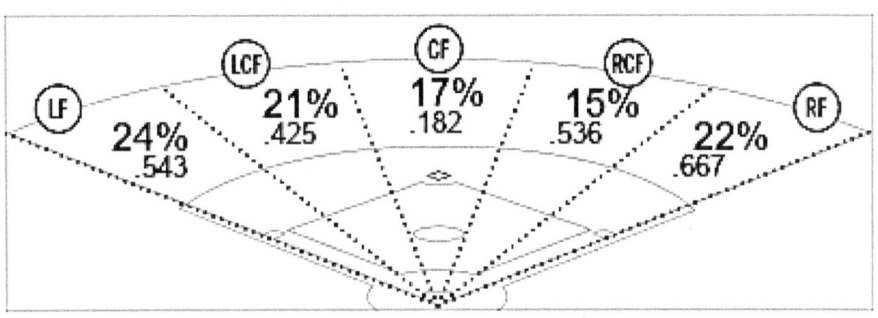

Strike Zone vs LHP   Strike Zone vs RHP

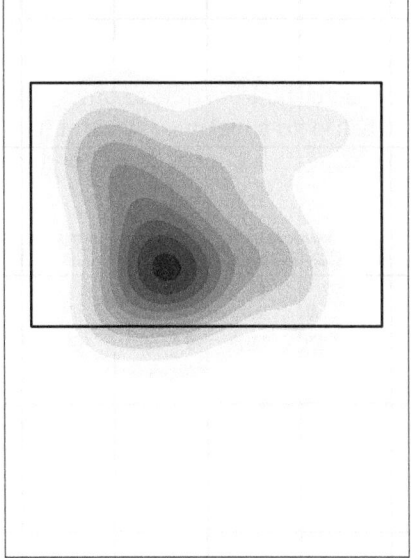

Charlie Culberson 3B

Born: 04/10/89 Age: 31 Bats: R Throws: R
Height: 6'0" Weight: 200 Origin: Round 1, 2007 Draft (#51 overall)

YEAR	TEAM	LVL	AGE	PA	R	2B	3B	HR	RBI	BB	K	SB	CS	AVG/OBP/SLG
2017	OKL	AAA	28	414	37	13	4	4	32	26	68	7	3	.250/.299/.336
2017	LAN	MLB	28	15	0	1	0	0	1	2	4	0	0	.154/.267/.231
2018	ATL	MLB	29	322	47	18	2	12	45	21	85	4	2	.270/.326/.466
2019	ATL	MLB	30	144	14	5	2	5	20	6	44	0	1	.259/.294/.437
2020	ATL	MLB	31	259	25	11	1	7	28	15	73	3	1	.237/.287/.379

Comparables: Danny Santana, Leury García, Aaron Boone

By day, the unassuming Culberson spends his time performing rudimentary utility duties and sending chills of slight disappointment down the spines of fans who walked up to him expecting an autograph from Dansby Swanson. However, the onset of night calls for Culberson to don the mask and become "Charlie Clutch." While the numbers suggest that he is just as unassuming as his alter ego, it is not Culberson who is out there making a game-winning defensive play by throwing across his body from the outfield to punch out a runner at home plate. Culberson is not the man who has a knack for coming through with a big pinch hit from time to time. Culberson is not the guy who has a 92-mph fastball in his shockingly live arm. The figure in the night accomplishing these unlikely feats is Charlie Clutch, and there's no telling what his next feat of legend will be.

YEAR	TEAM	LVL	AGE	PA	DRC+	VORP	BABIP	BRR	FRAA	WARP
2017	OKL	AAA	28	414	68	-3.8	.294	-0.6	SS(97): 0.8, 3B(7): 0.9	0.4
2017	LAN	MLB	28	15	84	-1.2	.222	0.0	SS(11): 0.2, 2B(2): 0.0	0.0
2018	ATL	MLB	29	322	101	22.2	.340	2.3	LF(29): -2.1, SS(20): -2.6	0.5
2019	ATL	MLB	30	144	75	0.2	.345	-0.2	LF(35): 1.9, RF(11): 1.1	0.3
2020	ATL	MLB	31	259	73	-1.0	.312	0.8	3B -1, 2B 0	-0.3

Charlie Culberson, continued

Batted Ball Distribution

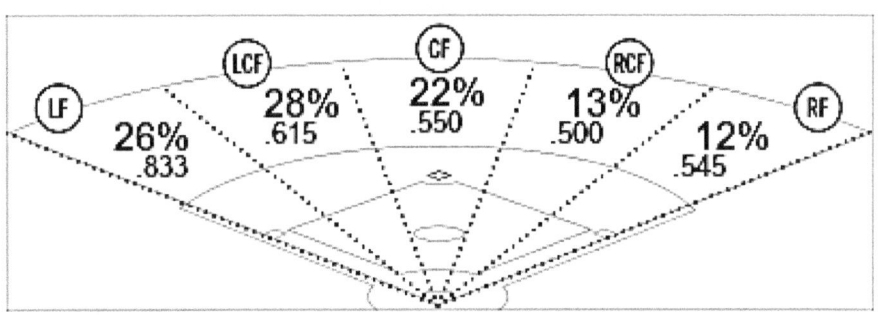

Strike Zone vs LHP   Strike Zone vs RHP

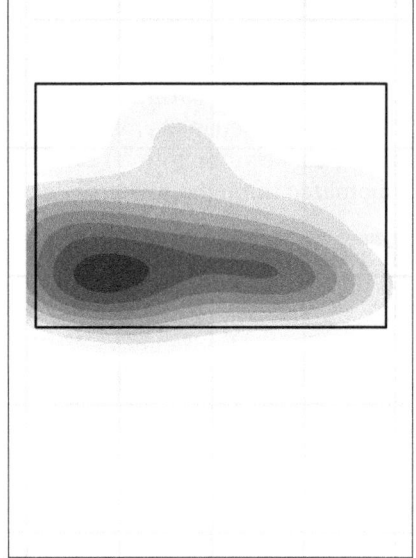

Atlanta Braves 2020

Adam Duvall   OF
Born: 09/04/88   Age: 31   Bats: R   Throws: R
Height: 6'1"   Weight: 215   Origin: Round 11, 2010 Draft (#348 overall)

YEAR	TEAM	LVL	AGE	PA	R	2B	3B	HR	RBI	BB	K	SB	CS	AVG/OBP/SLG
2017	CIN	MLB	28	647	78	37	3	31	99	39	170	5	3	.249/.301/.480
2018	CIN	MLB	29	370	40	19	0	15	61	34	100	2	2	.205/.286/.399
2018	ATL	MLB	29	57	8	1	0	0	0	3	17	0	0	.132/.193/.151
2019	GWN	AAA	30	429	74	20	4	32	93	48	86	1	0	.266/.364/.602
2019	ATL	MLB	30	130	17	4	1	10	19	7	39	0	0	.267/.315/.567
2020	ATL	MLB	31	210	28	10	1	13	34	16	59	2	1	.236/.304/.502

Comparables: Steve Balboni, Cecil Fielder, Al Ferrara

It was a banner year at the plate for Duvall in 2019, as he crushed fastball after fastball on his way to setting a team single-season record for home runs. Duvall even got to represent his team at the All-Star Game and the team duly rewarded him by naming him as their Most Valuable Player. That's an amazing year for anybody, but the fine print shows that it was done for the Gwinnett Stripers and not the Atlanta Braves. That's not where anybody expects to be for their age-30 season after putting three full seasons under their belt, but that's the situation Duvall found himself in after a career-worst 2018 season. Based on his strong close to the season in the majors, he's probably left the buses behind for good. That's great news for both his career and the careers of all those southpaws he demoralized throughout International League parks.

YEAR	TEAM	LVL	AGE	PA	DRC+	VORP	BABIP	BRR	FRAA	WARP
2017	CIN	MLB	28	647	99	24.4	.290	-2.2	LF(151): 6.7, 1B(3): 0.0	2.0
2018	CIN	MLB	29	370	81	3.3	.244	-0.6	LF(89): 6.9, 1B(10): 0.3	0.7
2018	ATL	MLB	29	57	83	-4.2	.194	0.6	LF(12): 0.0, RF(2): 0.0	0.1
2019	GWN	AAA	30	429	135	30.3	.261	0.2	LF(51): 4.7, RF(26): 1.5	3.1
2019	ATL	MLB	30	130	105	4.4	.306	0.4	LF(31): 1.8, RF(2): -0.5	0.6
2020	ATL	MLB	31	210	106	7.0	.268	-0.1	RF 0, LF 1	0.8

Adam Duvall, continued

Batted Ball Distribution

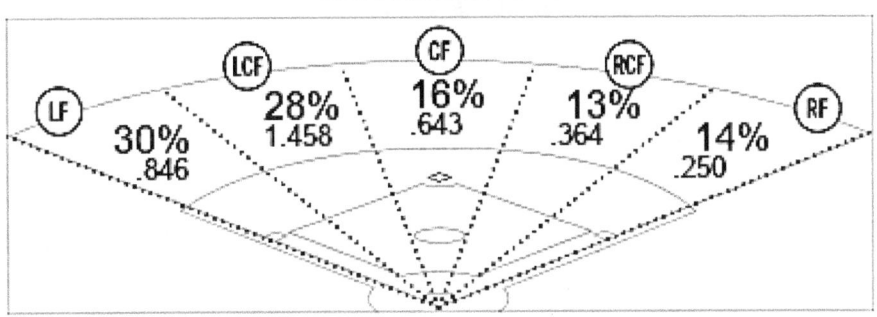

Strike Zone vs LHP   **Strike Zone vs RHP**

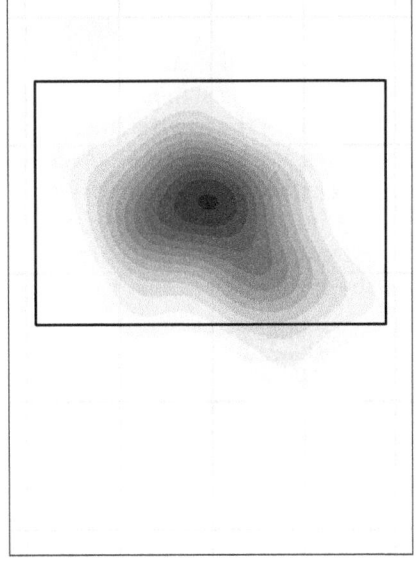

Tyler Flowers C

Born: 01/24/86 Age: 34 Bats: R Throws: R
Height: 6'4" Weight: 260 Origin: Round 33, 2005 Draft (#1007 overall)

YEAR	TEAM	LVL	AGE	PA	R	2B	3B	HR	RBI	BB	K	SB	CS	AVG/OBP/SLG
2017	ATL	MLB	31	370	41	16	0	12	49	31	82	0	1	.281/.378/.445
2018	ATL	MLB	32	296	34	9	0	8	30	35	76	0	0	.227/.341/.359
2019	ATL	MLB	33	310	36	11	3	11	34	31	105	0	0	.229/.319/.413
2020	ATL	MLB	34	322	35	14	1	10	37	28	108	1	0	.235/.321/.390

Comparables: Jarrod Saltalamacchia, Ramon Castro, Ron Karkovice

There are certain species of exotic flowers that are known for taking years, even decades, to bloom. The Giant Himalayan Lily has been known to take seven years before blooming. The Century Plant is actually a misnomer in that it can take as few as ten years before it reaches full bloom. As far as the baseball version goes, it took Flowers around nine seasons to bloom, as he put up a career year in 2017 at age 31. But comparing something beautiful against it's visual peak is the easiest way to lose sight of the fact that there's something you should treasure right in front of you. Yes, the DRC+ and FRAA are well down from his breakout, but an above-average catcher is hard to find. With a little positive regression in his contact within the strike zone—he dropped from above 70 percent in each of the last three seasons to a paltry 63 percent in 2019—Flowers could prove again to be worthy of admiration.

YEAR	TEAM	P. COUNT	FRM RUNS	BLK RUNS	THRW RUNS	TOT RUNS
2017	ATL	12424	32.0	-0.8	-1.1	30.1
2018	ATL	10185	13.7	-0.4	-0.2	13.0
2019	ATL	11720	15.3	-3.8	-0.6	10.7
2020	ATL	14576	15.2	-2.2	-0.6	12.4

YEAR	TEAM	LVL	AGE	PA	DRC+	VORP	BABIP	BRR	FRAA	WARP
2017	ATL	MLB	31	370	115	35.3	.342	-0.2	C(85): 29.5	5.5
2018	ATL	MLB	32	296	100	14.5	.292	0.3	C(76): 13.2	2.9
2019	ATL	MLB	33	310	79	8.0	.325	-3.7	C(83): 10.3	1.4
2020	ATL	MLB	34	322	87	9.0	.342	-0.8	C 12	2.2

Tyler Flowers, continued

Batted Ball Distribution

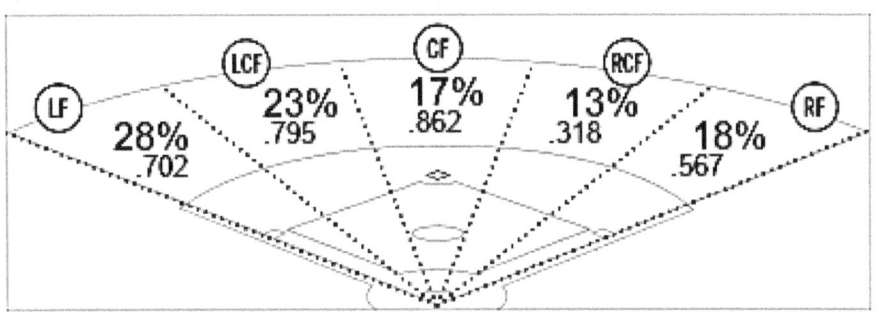

Strike Zone vs LHP **Strike Zone vs RHP**

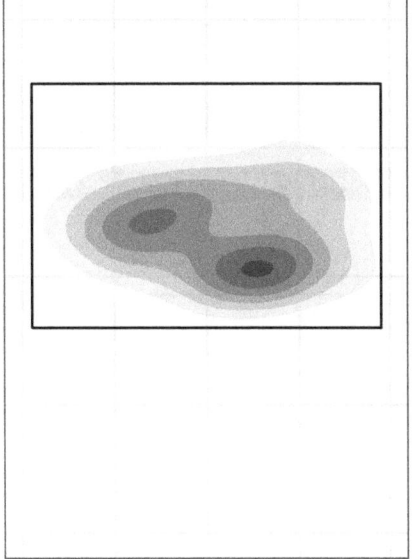

Freddie Freeman 1B

Born: 09/12/89 Age: 30 Bats: L Throws: R
Height: 6'5" Weight: 220 Origin: Round 2, 2007 Draft (#78 overall)

YEAR	TEAM	LVL	AGE	PA	R	2B	3B	HR	RBI	BB	K	SB	CS	AVG/OBP/SLG
2017	ATL	MLB	27	514	84	35	2	28	71	65	95	8	5	.307/.403/.586
2018	ATL	MLB	28	707	94	44	4	23	98	76	132	10	3	.309/.388/.505
2019	ATL	MLB	29	692	113	34	2	38	121	87	127	6	3	.295/.389/.549
2020	ATL	MLB	30	595	84	33	2	30	92	75	117	6	2	.285/.382/.529

Comparables: Paul Goldschmidt, Pat Burrell, Jason Thompson

In early 2014, an ice storm hit the Atlanta metro area and Freeman had the bad luck of being out in the middle of it. Chipper Jones rescued him from the Atlanta traffic armageddon and the picture of a grateful and gleeful Freeman clutching onto Chipper's back as they rode into a garage was immortalized with a bobblehead promotion. Freeman's look of gratefulness also reflects how he must feel batting in a lineup with weapons all around him. However, for the analogy to truly hold, Chipper would had to have floated in on a UH-60 Black Hawk. Freeman has had four consecutive elite offensive seasons and there are no signs of him slowing down anytime soon. In his age-30 season, there will be plenty more cold nights on the horizon for opposing pitchers and Freeman will be the one clearing the traffic on the bases with ease.

YEAR	TEAM	LVL	AGE	PA	DRC+	VORP	BABIP	BRR	FRAA	WARP
2017	ATL	MLB	27	514	145	52.9	.335	2.7	1B(105): -1.2, 3B(16): -2.4	3.7
2018	ATL	MLB	28	707	137	53.7	.358	-1.7	1B(161): 3.5	4.4
2019	ATL	MLB	29	692	141	47.9	.318	0.6	1B(158): -7.5	4.0
2020	ATL	MLB	30	595	135	39.5	.317	0.6	1B 0	4.1

Freddie Freeman, continued

Batted Ball Distribution

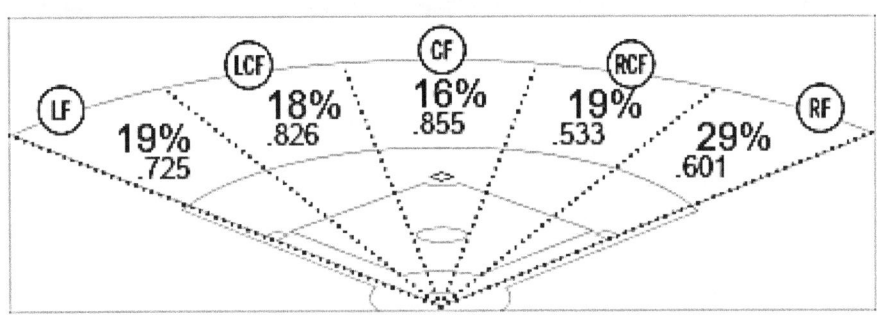

Strike Zone vs LHP **Strike Zone vs RHP**

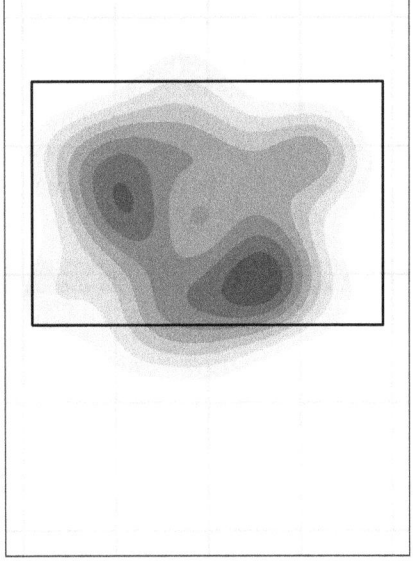

Adeiny Hechavarría INF
Born: 04/15/89   Age: 31   Bats: R   Throws: R
Height: 6'0"   Weight: 195   Origin: International Free Agent, 2010

YEAR	TEAM	LVL	AGE	PA	R	2B	3B	HR	RBI	BB	K	SB	CS	AVG/OBP/SLG
2017	JUP	A+	28	27	1	0	0	0	1	3	1	1	1	.304/.407/.304
2017	MIA	MLB	28	67	8	2	1	1	6	1	9	0	0	.277/.288/.385
2017	TBA	MLB	28	281	29	12	4	7	24	12	58	4	1	.257/.289/.411
2018	TBA	MLB	29	237	29	7	0	3	26	12	37	1	0	.258/.289/.332
2018	PIT	MLB	29	47	2	4	0	1	3	3	11	0	0	.233/.277/.395
2018	NYA	MLB	29	37	3	0	0	2	2	1	10	1	0	.194/.216/.361
2019	SYR	AAA	30	102	15	9	0	0	17	6	14	2	1	.348/.382/.446
2019	ATL	MLB	30	70	14	5	1	4	15	6	15	0	0	.328/.400/.639
2019	NYN	MLB	30	151	20	7	0	5	18	8	33	3	1	.204/.252/.359
2020	ATL	MLB	31	251	22	10	1	5	25	14	49	2	1	.232/.278/.355

Comparables: Mark Lewis, Hubie Brooks, Mike Lamb

Hechavarría has become a rolling stone, and wherever he flips his bat and lays down his glove is his home. The streets of New York were clearly too cold for him, as stints with both the Yankees and Mets ended up becoming disastrous, with the latter releasing him one day before he was set to receive a $1 million bonus. Hechavarría responded by signing with the Braves, publicly thanking God that he was released by the Mets, and then hitting two home runs as a visitor at Citi Field in the final game of the season. In the words of the wise sage Andre 3000, "what's cooler than being cool? Ice cold."

YEAR	TEAM	LVL	AGE	PA	DRC+	VORP	BABIP	BRR	FRAA	WARP
2017	JUP	A+	28	27	156	1.5	.318	-0.6	SS(8): 1.0	0.3
2017	MIA	MLB	28	67	83	0.6	.309	-0.9	SS(19): -1.1	0.0
2017	TBA	MLB	28	281	85	5.9	.302	-1.3	SS(77): 3.4	1.0
2018	TBA	MLB	29	237	89	6.5	.290	1.5	SS(61): -1.3	0.8
2018	PIT	MLB	29	47	88	-1.1	.281	-1.3	SS(15): -1.1	-0.1
2018	NYA	MLB	29	37	88	-0.2	.208	0.1	SS(16): -1.4, 3B(4): -0.3	-0.1
2019	SYR	AAA	30	102	123	7.4	.395	0.3	SS(14): 1.9, 3B(13): -1.1	0.8
2019	ATL	MLB	30	70	132	6.1	.372	0.4	SS(12): -0.2, 2B(3): -0.4	0.6
2019	NYN	MLB	30	151	73	0.4	.231	-1.8	2B(26): -1.6, SS(15): -0.2	-0.4
2020	ATL	MLB	31	251	66	-3.7	.273	-0.8	SS 0, 2B 0	-0.5

Adeiny Hechavarría, continued

Batted Ball Distribution

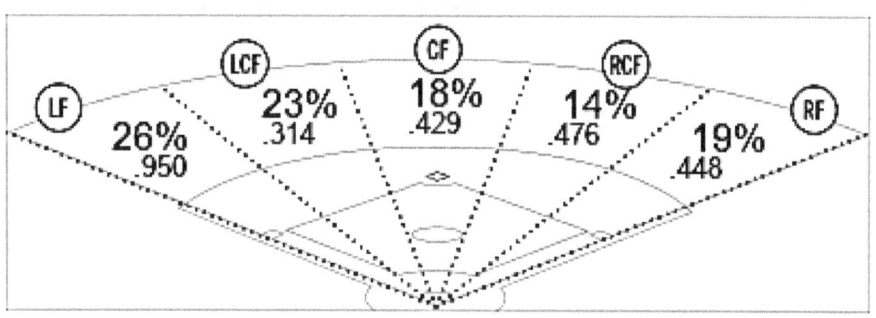

Strike Zone vs LHP **Strike Zone vs RHP**

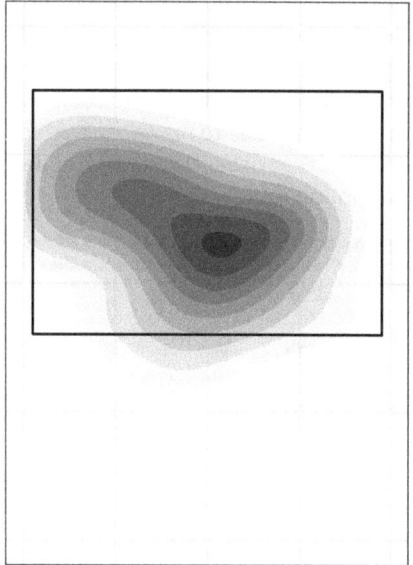

Ender Inciarte CF

Born: 10/29/90   Age: 29   Bats: L   Throws: L
Height: 5'11"   Weight: 190   Origin: International Free Agent, 2008

YEAR	TEAM	LVL	AGE	PA	R	2B	3B	HR	RBI	BB	K	SB	CS	AVG/OBP/SLG
2017	ATL	MLB	26	718	93	27	5	11	57	49	94	22	9	.304/.350/.409
2018	ATL	MLB	27	660	83	27	6	10	61	49	86	28	14	.265/.325/.380
2019	GWN	AAA	28	30	5	1	0	0	1	4	3	0	1	.231/.333/.269
2019	ATL	MLB	28	230	30	11	2	5	24	26	41	7	1	.246/.343/.397
2020	ATL	MLB	29	504	48	22	3	8	48	40	82	15	7	.252/.315/.368

Comparables: Coco Crisp, Melky Cabrera, Michael Brantley

Whenever Inciarte takes the field, he's going to produce. Being known as a defensive specialist who hits just enough to justify being an everyday player may not be a glamorous profile, but it's a useful one to have in your team's toolbox. Sadly, Inciarte wasn't able to get a lot of time on the field last season, as a back injury and a hamstring injury limited him to just 230 plate appearances. But even a smaller sample size than normal did nothing to diminish the incredible consistency that the lefty has shown, as he's settled in as just below average by DRC+ every season of his career. Given the Braves' roster construction and the 100-point dip he takes when facing a same-side arm, Inciarte continues to make the perfect platoon center fielder and remains under contract for another three years at a very reasonable $24 million (assuming his 2022 option is picked up).

YEAR	TEAM	LVL	AGE	PA	DRC+	VORP	BABIP	BRR	FRAA	WARP
2017	ATL	MLB	26	718	98	34.8	.339	5.4	CF(156): 10.4	3.9
2018	ATL	MLB	27	660	95	25.7	.293	2.3	CF(155): 9.6	3.1
2019	GWN	AAA	28	30	86	-0.4	.261	0.3	CF(5): 0.1	0.1
2019	ATL	MLB	28	230	95	7.1	.286	0.4	CF(63): 4.5	1.2
2020	ATL	MLB	29	504	81	8.3	.291	2.0	CF 8	1.7

Ender Inciarte, continued

Batted Ball Distribution

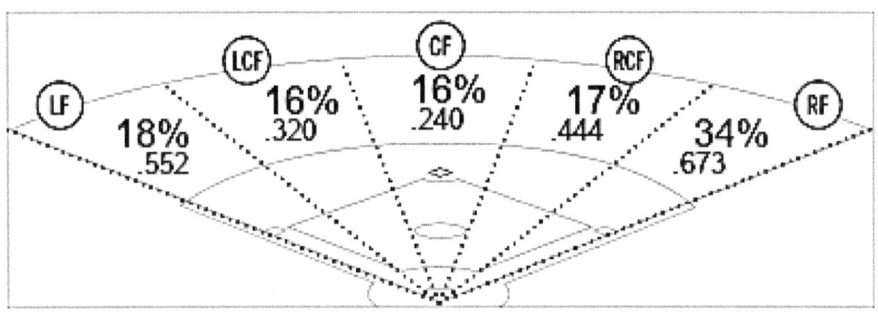

Strike Zone vs LHP   Strike Zone vs RHP

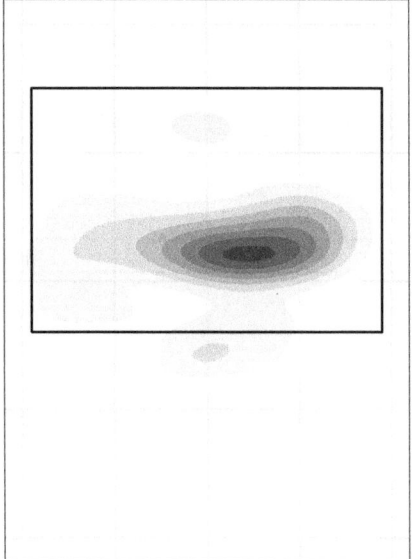

Braves Player Analysis - 33

Nick Markakis RF

Born: 11/17/83 Age: 36 Bats: L Throws: L
Height: 6'1" Weight: 210 Origin: Round 1, 2003 Draft (#7 overall)

YEAR	TEAM	LVL	AGE	PA	R	2B	3B	HR	RBI	BB	K	SB	CS	AVG/OBP/SLG
2017	ATL	MLB	33	670	76	39	1	8	76	68	110	0	2	.275/.354/.384
2018	ATL	MLB	34	705	78	43	2	14	93	72	80	1	1	.297/.366/.440
2019	ATL	MLB	35	469	61	25	2	9	62	47	59	2	0	.285/.356/.420
2020	ATL	MLB	36	560	56	33	1	10	57	53	83	1	1	.267/.341/.395

Comparables: Denard Span, Al Cowens, Claudell Washington

After delivering a shockingly good contract year in which he outproduced the first three years of his four-year pact with the Braves, Markakis had earned a shot to show that his one season of glory wasn't a flash in the pan. Break out your best Ron Howard voice because it was. His value to a clubhouse is still extremely high and if you ask any of his teammates or casual fans about him, they will speak about him in wistful tones. That kind of clout goes a long way and while Markakis may not do much to separate himself from replacement level as he barrels towards his late 30s, he's still immaculate when it comes to intangibles.

YEAR	TEAM	LVL	AGE	PA	DRC+	VORP	BABIP	BRR	FRAA	WARP
2017	ATL	MLB	33	670	95	20.1	.324	2.1	RF(156): -9.0	0.3
2018	ATL	MLB	34	705	116	34.4	.318	-1.6	RF(158): 6.9, LF(3): -0.4	3.5
2019	ATL	MLB	35	469	106	14.9	.310	-2.8	RF(103): -11.5, LF(9): 3.4	0.4
2020	ATL	MLB	36	560	95	10.4	.304	-0.5	LF 1, RF 0	1.1

Nick Markakis, continued

Batted Ball Distribution

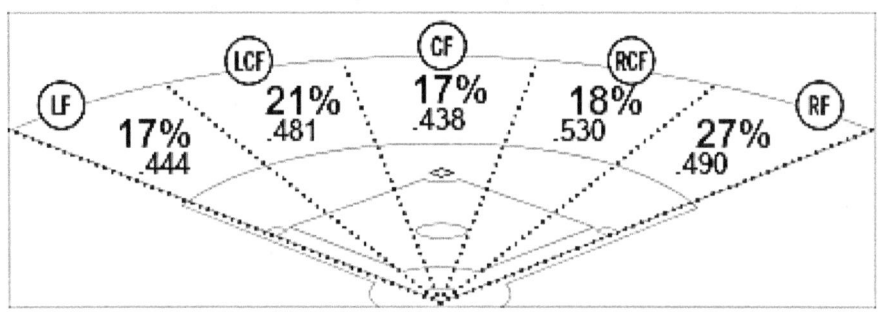

Strike Zone vs LHP   **Strike Zone vs RHP**

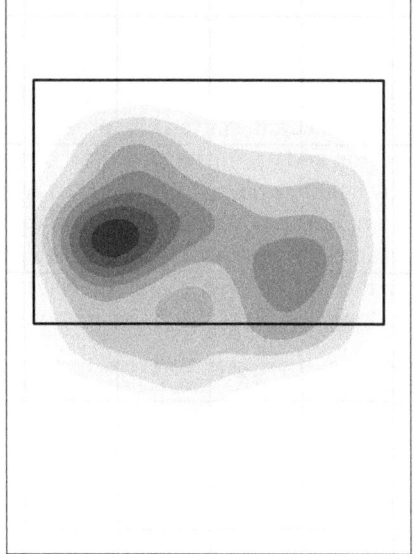

Brian McCann C

Born: 02/20/84   Age: 36   Bats: L   Throws: R
Height: 6'3"   Weight: 225   Origin: Round 2, 2002 Draft (#64 overall)

YEAR	TEAM	LVL	AGE	PA	R	2B	3B	HR	RBI	BB	K	SB	CS	AVG/OBP/SLG
2017	HOU	MLB	33	399	47	12	1	18	62	38	58	1	0	.241/.323/.436
2018	HOU	MLB	34	216	22	3	0	7	23	19	40	0	1	.212/.301/.339
2019	ATL	MLB	35	316	28	9	0	12	45	31	53	0	0	.249/.323/.412
2020	ATL	MLB	36	251	28	10	0	9	31	23	48	1	0	.235/.315/.407

Comparables: Lance Parrish, Johnny Edwards, Mike Macfarlane

YEAR	TEAM	P. COUNT	FRM RUNS	BLK RUNS	THRW RUNS	TOT RUNS
2017	HOU	13673	1.4	-0.4	-2.5	-1.7
2018	HOU	7671	-3.0	-1.4	0.1	-4.5
2019	ATL	11106	5.3	-0.9	-0.7	3.4
2020	ATL	11770	-0.9	-0.3	-0.8	-2.0

In 2005, the Braves were at the end of their divisional dynasty that started in the early 1990s and stretched until a 21-year-old McCann was ready to make his debut, compiling 59 appearances as a rookie. By the time 2019 rolled around, McCann was back with the Braves for one last run at a division. All of his teammates from that 2005 team were now on the sidelines and one of them (namely, Jeff Francoeur) was in the press box to watch McCann play the final 85 games of his career for the Braves. McCann started his career as part of an Atlanta team that won their division and he finished it as part of an Atlanta team that won their division. It may not have been the Hollywood ending of another World Series championship that McCann had wanted, but ending a fantastic career with your baseball life coming full circle in the postseason isn't a bad note to end on. To top it all off, he even posted the exact same DRC+ in both his first and final seasons. Time is a flat circle and nobody can tell you that better than McCann.

YEAR	TEAM	LVL	AGE	PA	DRC+	VORP	BABIP	BRR	FRAA	WARP
2017	HOU	MLB	33	399	106	19.5	.237	-0.2	C(95): -2.6	2.0
2018	HOU	MLB	34	216	96	3.9	.229	-1.5	C(62): -3.4	0.5
2019	ATL	MLB	35	316	100	16.8	.261	-3.7	C(83): 5.0	1.8
2020	ATL	MLB	36	251	91	4.1	.261	-1.1	C -2	0.3

Brian McCann, continued

Batted Ball Distribution

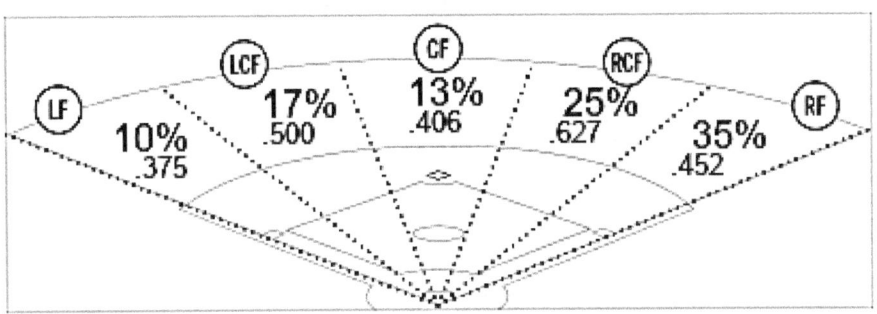

Strike Zone vs LHP

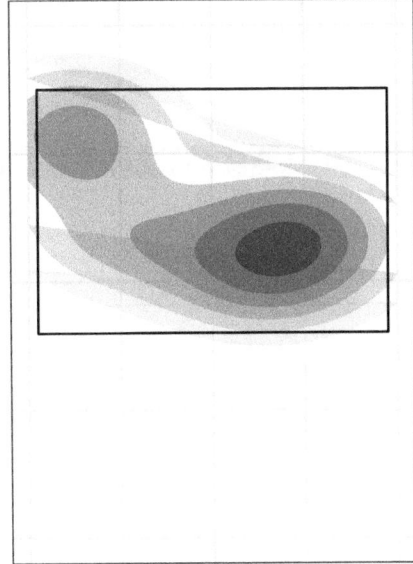

Strike Zone vs RHP

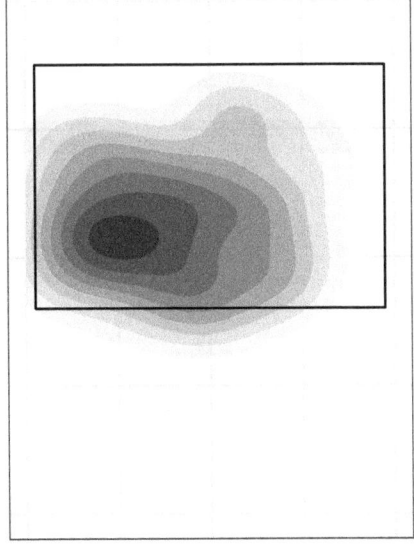

Marcell Ozuna LF

Born: 11/12/90 Age: 29 Bats: R Throws: R
Height: 6'1" Weight: 225 Origin: International Free Agent, 2008

YEAR	TEAM	LVL	AGE	PA	R	2B	3B	HR	RBI	BB	K	SB	CS	AVG/OBP/SLG
2017	MIA	MLB	26	679	93	30	2	37	124	64	144	1	3	.312/.376/.548
2018	SLN	MLB	27	628	69	16	2	23	88	38	110	3	0	.280/.325/.433
2019	SLN	MLB	28	549	80	23	1	29	89	62	114	12	2	.243/.330/.474
2020	SLN	MLB	29	550	70	23	2	28	81	50	122	2	1	.258/.328/.477

Comparables: Andruw Jones, Glenallen Hill, Kevin Kiermaier

Ozuna entered the winter possessing a rare pairing of qualities: he was young for a free agent, having just completed his age-28 season, and having already produced a star-level season in his past. Alas, that season was 2017 rather than 2019, and some of his value that year came from strong defense, which is emphatically no longer the case. But, despite those downsides, there's untapped potential here. Ozuna has crushed the ball the last two years, albeit without having the results to show for it. He graded well when judged by ball-tracking metrics in 2019, and posted a career-high walk rate and career-low chase rate. Has Ozuna peaked? Perhaps, but it seems like the baseball gods owe him a career year based on his under-the-hood numbers.

YEAR	TEAM	LVL	AGE	PA	DRC+	VORP	BABIP	BRR	FRAA	WARP
2017	MIA	MLB	26	679	134	55.1	.355	-3.5	LF(152): 4.9, CF(3): 0.0	4.8
2018	SLN	MLB	27	628	109	30.9	.309	2.6	LF(147): -2.2	2.4
2019	SLN	MLB	28	549	111	23.4	.259	3.1	LF(129): -11.2	1.5
2020	SLN	MLB	29	550	109	11.3	.290	0.3	LF -2, CF 0	2.4

Marcell Ozuna, continued

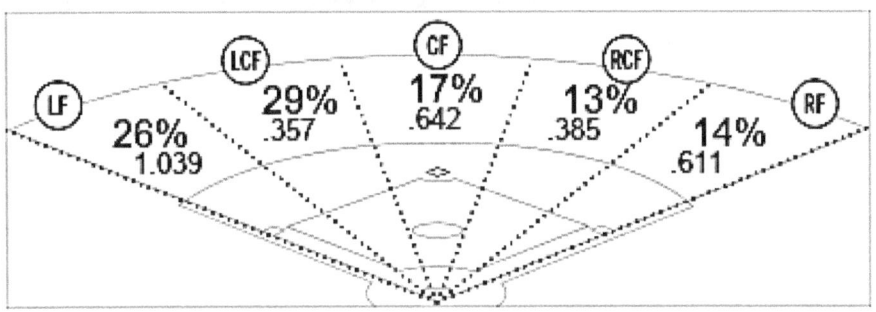

Strike Zone vs LHP   **Strike Zone vs RHP**

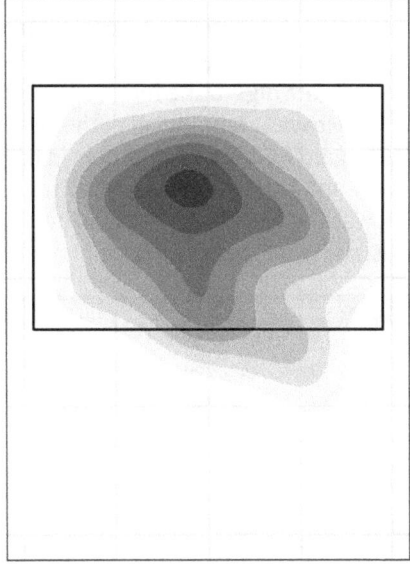

Austin Riley 3B/OF

Born: 04/02/97 Age: 23 Bats: R Throws: R
Height: 6'3" Weight: 220 Origin: Round 1, 2015 Draft (#41 overall)

YEAR	TEAM	LVL	AGE	PA	R	2B	3B	HR	RBI	BB	K	SB	CS	AVG/OBP/SLG
2017	BRV	A+	20	339	43	10	1	12	47	23	74	0	2	.252/.310/.408
2017	MIS	AA	20	203	28	9	1	8	27	20	50	2	0	.315/.389/.511
2018	MIS	AA	21	109	17	10	3	6	20	8	28	0	0	.333/.394/.677
2018	GWN	AAA	21	324	41	17	0	12	47	26	95	1	0	.282/.346/.464
2019	GWN	AAA	22	194	39	13	0	15	41	20	39	0	0	.293/.366/.626
2019	ATL	MLB	22	297	41	11	1	18	49	16	108	0	2	.226/.279/.471
2020	ATL	MLB	23	539	69	25	1	31	85	36	178	1	0	.243/.301/.487

Comparables: Clint Frazier, Javier Báez, Mike Moustakas

Imagine being a kid and being told two things. First, you get to go to a candy store. Next, you get to do whatever you want in that candy store for a limited amount of time but then the grown-ups will have to come in and take care of you once your time is up. The kid probably wouldn't care about anything that was said to them after "whatever you want in that candy store," and they would just proceed to run as wild as humanly possible. That's what Riley did for his 30 games in the bigs, as he hit .298/.336/.628 with 11 home runs and a whopping 32 RBI. He was grabbing all of the sweets and tearing through each bag with little regard for himself or others in his path. Then the alarm went off. The grown-ups found out that he had trouble with anything other than a fastball and that was the end, for now. When he's older and figures out how to hit breaking balls, the whole league will be his candy store.

YEAR	TEAM	LVL	AGE	PA	DRC+	VORP	BABIP	BRR	FRAA	WARP
2017	BRV	A+	20	339	111	13.6	.289	-0.4	3B(80): -2.5	1.1
2017	MIS	AA	20	203	156	20.0	.393	-0.5	3B(47): -1.6	1.6
2018	MIS	AA	21	109	179	19.1	.415	1.0	3B(27): 1.2	1.5
2018	GWN	AAA	21	324	127	24.1	.374	1.1	3B(71): -0.3	2.0
2019	GWN	AAA	22	194	139	15.8	.300	0.2	3B(30): -0.9, LF(7): -0.8	1.3
2019	ATL	MLB	22	297	89	3.9	.293	-0.4	LF(58): 2.0, 1B(6): -0.8	0.4
2020	ATL	MLB	23	539	100	13.8	.311	0.5	3B -1, LF -1	1.3

Austin Riley, continued

Batted Ball Distribution

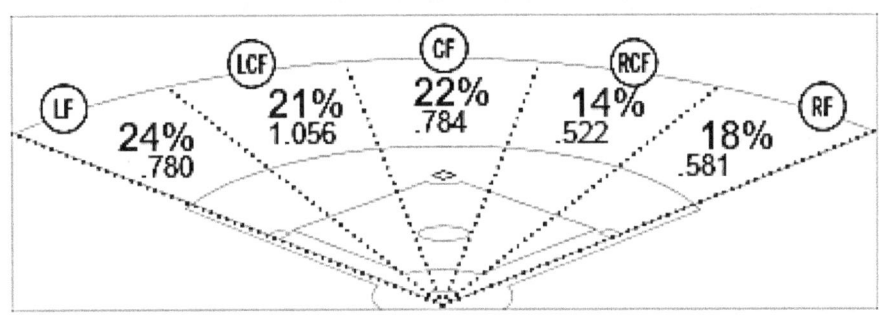

Strike Zone vs LHP   **Strike Zone vs RHP**

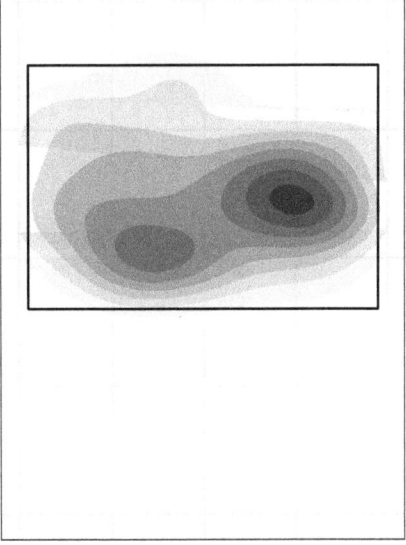

Atlanta Braves 2020

Dansby Swanson SS
Born: 02/11/94 Age: 26 Bats: R Throws: R
Height: 6'1" Weight: 190 Origin: Round 1, 2015 Draft (#1 overall)

YEAR	TEAM	LVL	AGE	PA	R	2B	3B	HR	RBI	BB	K	SB	CS	AVG/OBP/SLG
2017	GWN	AAA	23	45	5	1	0	1	5	6	9	1	0	.237/.356/.342
2017	ATL	MLB	23	551	59	23	2	6	51	59	120	3	3	.232/.312/.324
2018	ATL	MLB	24	533	51	25	4	14	59	44	122	10	4	.238/.304/.395
2019	ATL	MLB	25	545	77	26	3	17	65	51	124	10	5	.251/.325/.422
2020	ATL	MLB	26	595	64	27	3	17	68	56	139	7	3	.244/.320/.403

Comparables: Eugenio Suárez, Everth Cabrera, Rico Petrocelli

When the universe conspires to give someone like Swanson a series of events that includes the honor of being the first overall pick in his draft class, getting traded to his hometown team and building a stadium that casts a shadow on your stomping grounds, exterior expectations can go through the roof. The fans were sold on a player who could be the star of a bright future while in a dark and murky present. His handsome face was on billboards and commercials across the metro area. In actuality, Swanson had the profile of a shortstop who could be a steady rock in the middle of the diamond and a calming presence in the lower third of the lineup. In short, he's a good everyday player who you can trust not to disappoint or overwhelm you. The bright lights of hometown fame may have dimmed a bit but if anybody is proof that you can always go home and lead a steady life, it's Swanson.

YEAR	TEAM	LVL	AGE	PA	DRC+	VORP	BABIP	BRR	FRAA	WARP
2017	GWN	AAA	23	45	97	1.5	.286	-0.9	SS(9): -0.9, 2B(2): -0.2	0.0
2017	ATL	MLB	23	551	77	12.8	.292	3.2	SS(142): -10.1	0.2
2018	ATL	MLB	24	533	91	23.1	.290	0.9	SS(136): 5.4	2.5
2019	ATL	MLB	25	545	97	24.5	.300	1.6	SS(126): 1.3	2.7
2020	ATL	MLB	26	595	90	17.1	.298	2.1	SS -1	1.6

Dansby Swanson, continued

Batted Ball Distribution

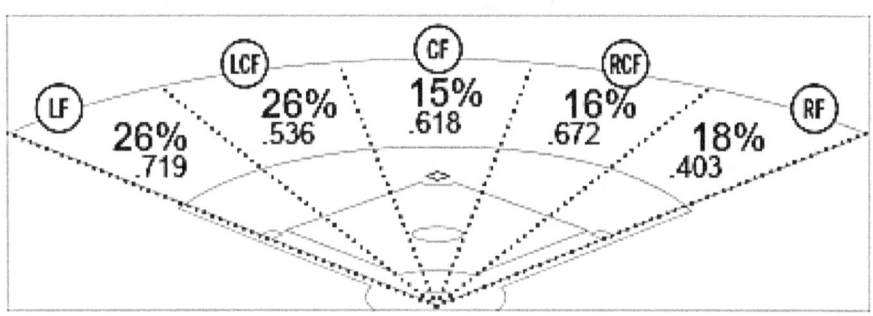

Strike Zone vs LHP

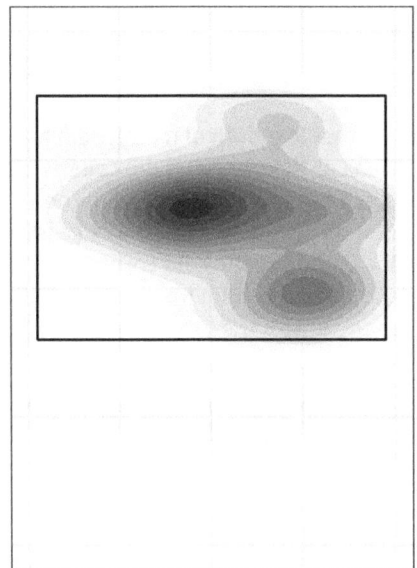

Strike Zone vs RHP

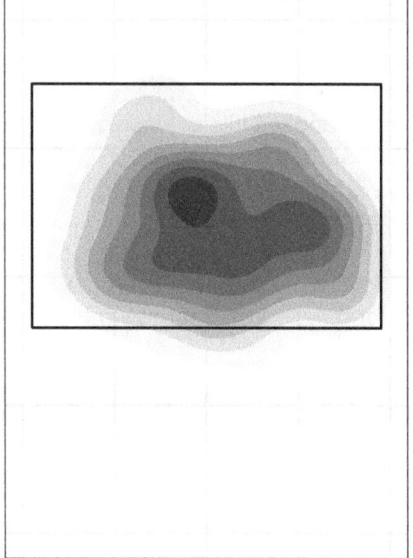

Travis d'Arnaud   C

Born: 02/10/89   Age: 31   Bats: R   Throws: R
Height: 6'2"   Weight: 210   Origin: Round 1, 2007 Draft (#37 overall)

YEAR	TEAM	LVL	AGE	PA	R	2B	3B	HR	RBI	BB	K	SB	CS	AVG/OBP/SLG
2017	NYN	MLB	28	376	39	19	1	16	57	23	59	0	0	.244/.293/.443
2018	NYN	MLB	29	16	1	0	0	1	3	1	5	0	0	.200/.250/.400
2019	LAN	MLB	30	1	0	0	0	0	0	0	0	0	0	.000/.000/.000
2019	TBA	MLB	30	365	50	16	0	16	67	30	80	0	1	.263/.323/.459
2019	NYN	MLB	30	25	2	0	0	0	2	2	5	0	0	.087/.160/.087
2020	ATL	MLB	31	294	32	14	0	11	37	23	61	0	0	.248/.313/.422

Comparables: Gary Carter, Bill Freehan, Jim Pagliaroni

It was quite the year for d'Arnaud. He started another season with the Mets before they designated him for assignment out of frustration in late April after a 2-for-23 start at the plate. Los Angeles took a flier on him; though he wore Dodger blue just once before the Rays came calling for help. At the time, he looked like a temporary fix for a team that lost both of its catchers to injury at the same time. Meanwhile, a hot streak at the plate and the collapse of Mike Zunino, allowed for a larger role. The LBC native took advantage of the opportunity and became Tampa Bay's primary backstop for most of the season. He even hit his way into a platoon at first base, handling the cold corner and leadoff position against southpaws. The resurgence took him from a potential minor-league contract this winter to two-year deal with the Braves for $16 million.

YEAR	TEAM	P. COUNT	FRM RUNS	BLK RUNS	THRW RUNS	TOT RUNS
2017	NYN	13404	11.2	0.9	-3.1	9.0
2018	NYN	689	1.0	0.1	0.0	1.0
2019	NYN	899	0.2	0.0	0.0	0.2
2019	TBA	9678	1.8	-2.4	0.1	-0.8
2020	ATL	13793	9.5	-0.3	0.1	9.3

YEAR	TEAM	LVL	AGE	PA	DRC+	VORP	BABIP	BRR	FRAA	WARP
2017	NYN	MLB	28	376	99	15.8	.250	-2.2	C(93): 11.5, 2B(1): 0.0	2.7
2018	NYN	MLB	29	16	80	0.7	.222	-0.1	C(4): 1.0	0.1
2019	LAN	MLB	30	1	105	0.0	.000	0.0		0.0
2019	TBA	MLB	30	365	104	17.6	.295	0.4	C(76): -2.2, 1B(21): -1.6	1.4
2019	NYN	MLB	30	25	70	0.4	.111	0.4	C(9): 0.1	0.1
2020	ATL	MLB	31	294	91	10.1	.285	-0.3	C 10	2.0

Travis d'Arnaud, continued

Batted Ball Distribution

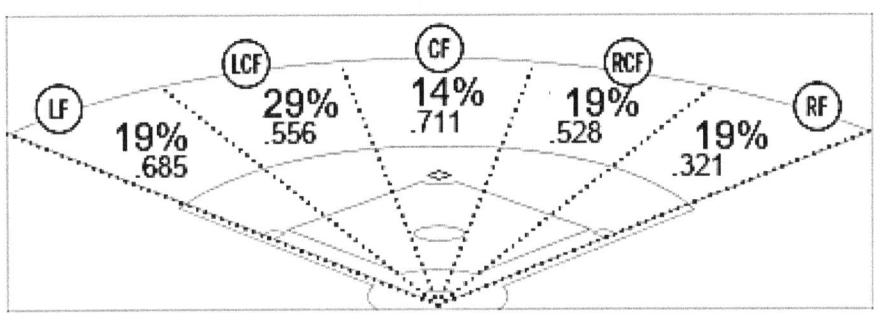

Strike Zone vs LHP   **Strike Zone vs RHP**

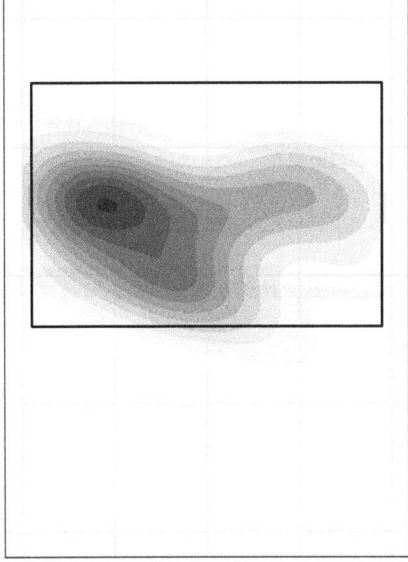

Mike Foltynewicz   RHP

Born: 10/07/91 Age: 28 Bats: R Throws: R
Height: 6'4" Weight: 200 Origin: Round 1, 2010 Draft (#19 overall)

YEAR	TEAM	LVL	AGE	W	L	SV	G	GS	IP	H	HR	BB/9	K/9	K	GB%	BABIP
2017	ATL	MLB	25	10	13	0	29	28	154	169	20	3.4	8.4	143	42%	.324
2018	ATL	MLB	26	13	10	0	31	31	183	130	17	3.3	9.9	202	44%	.251
2019	GWN	AAA	27	5	1	0	10	10	51^1	49	1	3.0	7.9	45	40%	.316
2019	ATL	MLB	27	8	6	0	21	21	117	109	23	2.8	8.1	105	39%	.265
2020	ATL	MLB	28	9	9	0	26	26	145	139	23	3.2	8.6	139	39%	.289

Comparables: Kevin Gausman, A.J. Cole, Joe Ross

There are few pitchers who had a more polarizing season than Foltynewicz. Just one year after seemingly breaking out and being on his way to becoming a viable frontline starter, his one step forward in 2018 resulted in 22 steps backward last season. A combination of limited spring training reps, poor performance and an equally poor in-game mentality resulted in Folty going from the penthouse of a major-league rotation to the outhouse of Triple-A baseball. Once he returned to the bigs with a new mindset—he would often let a single or a walk signal the end of the world—Foltynewicz's performance was more like the 2018 version rather than the 2019 version. Of course he didn't quite end the season on the best note, putting up the worst start in franchise playoff history (ex Tom Glavine division) in the NLDS winner-take-all game against the Cardinals. Sometimes your greatest enemy is yourself, and nobody knows that better than Foltynewicz now does.

YEAR	TEAM	LVL	AGE	WHIP	ERA	DRA	WARP	MPH	FB%	WHF	CSP
2017	ATL	MLB	25	1.48	4.79	5.52	0.1	98.3	60.7	10.3	46.6
2018	ATL	MLB	26	1.08	2.85	3.44	3.9	99.1	56.3	11.1	49
2019	GWN	AAA	27	1.29	3.86	3.67	1.5				
2019	ATL	MLB	27	1.25	4.54	4.36	1.8	97.4	52.2	11.4	50.4
2020	ATL	MLB	28	1.31	4.17	4.34	2.4	97.7	56.6	11.1	49.3

Mike Foltynewicz, continued

Pitch Shape vs LHH

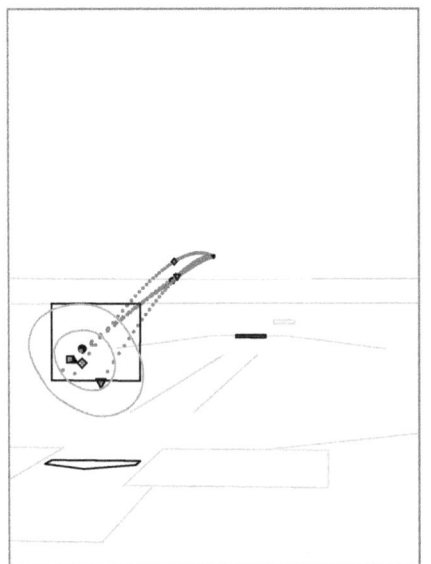

Pitch Shape vs RHH

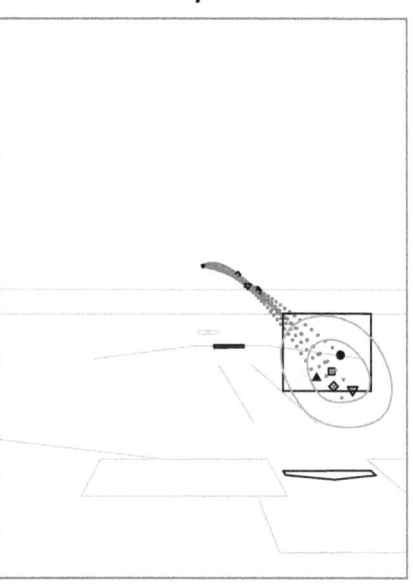

Type	Frequency	Velocity	H Movement	V Movement
● Fastball	26.4%	95 [107]	-7.7 [96]	-13.4 [107]
☐ Sinker	25.7%	95.1 [113]	-13.6 [94]	-18 [108]
+ Cutter				
▲ Changeup	9.4%	86.9 [106]	-12.2 [95]	-22.7 [114]
✕ Splitter				
▽ Slider	28.8%	85.5 [105]	3.4 [93]	-29.5 [110]
◇ Curveball	9.7%	79.5 [103]	4.3 [87]	-41.7 [112]
⊕ Slow Curveball				
✱ Knuckleball				
▼ Screwball				

Braves Player Analysis - 47

Atlanta Braves 2020

Max Fried   LHP
Born: 01/18/94   Age: 26   Bats: L   Throws: L
Height: 6'4"   Weight: 190   Origin: Round 1, 2012 Draft (#7 overall)

YEAR	TEAM	LVL	AGE	W	L	SV	G	GS	IP	H	HR	BB/9	K/9	K	GB%	BABIP
2017	MIS	AA	23	2	11	0	19	19	86^2	88	8	4.5	8.8	85	53%	.331
2017	GWN	AAA	23	0	0	0	2	2	6	1	0	3.0	9.0	6	67%	.083
2017	ATL	MLB	23	1	1	0	9	4	26	30	3	4.2	7.6	22	65%	.338
2018	MIS	AA	24	1	0	0	2	2	11^1	4	0	3.2	12.7	16	67%	.190
2018	GWN	AAA	24	2	6	0	13	13	66^1	66	4	4.1	9.6	71	58%	.343
2018	ATL	MLB	24	1	4	0	14	5	33^2	26	3	5.3	11.8	44	53%	.315
2019	ATL	MLB	25	17	6	0	33	30	165^2	174	21	2.6	9.4	173	55%	.336
2020	ATL	MLB	26	8	8	0	24	24	134	133	15	3.4	9.8	145	54%	.324

Comparables: Blake Snell, Felix Doubront, Chris Archer

The story of Fried has long been one of being the bridesmaid and not the bride. When he was the seventh-overall pick out of the draft in 2012, he was the second-best prospect taken in his high school rotation. And when Fried finally had his breakout season in 2019, it was far less heralded than the one his former teammate Lucas Giolito had on the South Side of Chicago. After making more than 60 percent of his MLB appearances between 2017 and 2018 out of the bullpen, Fried was a rock for the Braves, finishing second on the team behind Julio Teheran with 30 starts last season. And when he pitched, he excelled as his DRA and WARP were both second among starters on the team behind fellow youngster Mike Soroka. The two biggest reasons for his expanded success in 2019 was the development of his slider, which gave him a second bat-missing breaker to go with his curve that was fawned over as an amateur, and the fact that he held his velocity gains as he moved back into a full-time starter role. If that sounds like a pitcher who shouldn't play second fiddle to anyone, you're not wrong, but at least Fried is used to it.

YEAR	TEAM	LVL	AGE	WHIP	ERA	DRA	WARP	MPH	FB%	WHF	CSP
2017	MIS	AA	23	1.51	5.92	6.11	-1.0				
2017	GWN	AAA	23	0.50	0.00	2.51	0.2				
2017	ATL	MLB	23	1.62	3.81	4.79	0.2	95.5	63	9.2	45.4
2018	MIS	AA	24	0.71	0.00	1.80	0.5				
2018	GWN	AAA	24	1.45	4.61	4.93	0.5				
2018	ATL	MLB	24	1.37	2.94	3.31	0.7	96.7	58.7	14.4	48.1
2019	ATL	MLB	25	1.33	4.02	3.42	4.2	96.3	56.9	12.2	48.2
2020	ATL	MLB	26	1.37	4.06	4.15	2.5	95.9	58.7	12.5	48.3

Max Fried, continued

Pitch Shape vs LHH

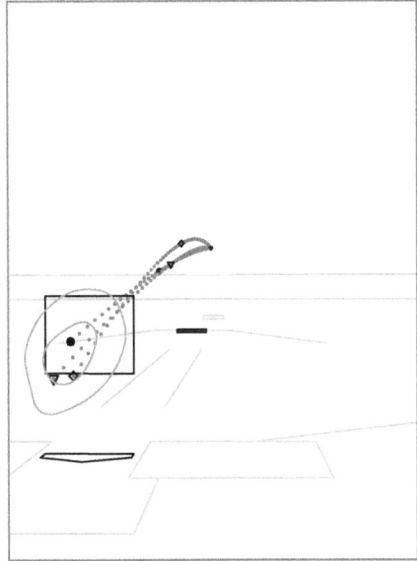

Pitch Shape vs RHH

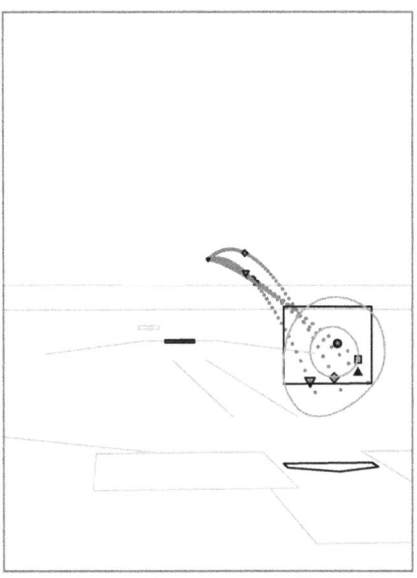

Type	Frequency	Velocity	H Movement	V Movement
● Fastball	54.0%	93.9 [104]	3.1 [117]	-16.5 [98]
☐ Sinker				
+ Cutter				
▲ Changeup				
✕ Splitter				
▽ Slider	16.0%	83.7 [97]	-10.8 [124]	-37 [89]
◇ Curveball	24.7%	74.6 [87]	-7.8 [101]	-61.2 [71]
⊕ Slow Curveball				
✱ Knuckleball				
▼ Screwball				

Atlanta Braves 2020

Shane Greene   RHP
Born: 11/17/88   Age: 31   Bats: R   Throws: R
Height: 6'4"   Weight: 197   Origin: Round 15, 2009 Draft (#465 overall)

YEAR	TEAM	LVL	AGE	W	L	SV	G	GS	IP	H	HR	BB/9	K/9	K	GB%	BABIP
2017	DET	MLB	28	4	3	9	71	0	67²	50	6	4.5	9.7	73	49%	.265
2018	DET	MLB	29	4	6	32	66	0	63¹	68	12	2.7	9.2	65	42%	.311
2019	ATL	MLB	30	0	1	1	27	0	24²	25	3	1.8	7.7	21	38%	.314
2019	DET	MLB	30	0	2	22	38	0	38	21	5	2.8	10.2	43	55%	.178
2020	ATL	MLB	31	2	2	6	48	0	51	50	8	3.1	9.2	52	45%	.303

Comparables: Roenis Elías, Joe Kelly, Neftalí Feliz

It was only a matter of time before Greene would be getting high-leverage opportunities in games that actually mattered after spending 2017 and 2018 racking up saves for the rebuilding Tigers. Sure enough, Greene found himself moving from the relative anonymity of pitching with nothing on the line in August to being thrust into a pennant race with the Braves. In professional wrestling, wrestlers who are still new to the big time and can't yet be trusted with a big match are considered to be green. After two blown saves and a loss in his first five appearances with Atlanta, you may have heard some rumblings of Greene being exactly this. However, in his final 22 games with the Braves, he pitched like the player Alex Anthopolous thought he was acquiring with a 2.61 ERA and proper ownership of the eighth inning. Not everybody can handle the main event role of the ninth inning, and Greene won't he asked to do so in 2020, but it's certainly premature to take the Proven Closer sticker off his post-2020 free agent spec sheet.

YEAR	TEAM	LVL	AGE	WHIP	ERA	DRA	WARP	MPH	FB%	WHF	CSP
2017	DET	MLB	28	1.24	2.66	4.56	0.5	96.8	56.2	9.8	52
2018	DET	MLB	29	1.37	5.12	3.94	0.7	96.4	50.8	9.9	51.1
2019	ATL	MLB	30	1.22	4.01	4.37	0.3	93.5	43.3	12.6	49.3
2019	DET	MLB	30	0.87	1.18	3.19	0.9	94.6	43.3	11.6	52.5
2020	ATL	MLB	31	1.32	4.26	4.40	0.6	94.7	49	10.6	51.1

Shane Greene, continued

Pitch Shape vs LHH

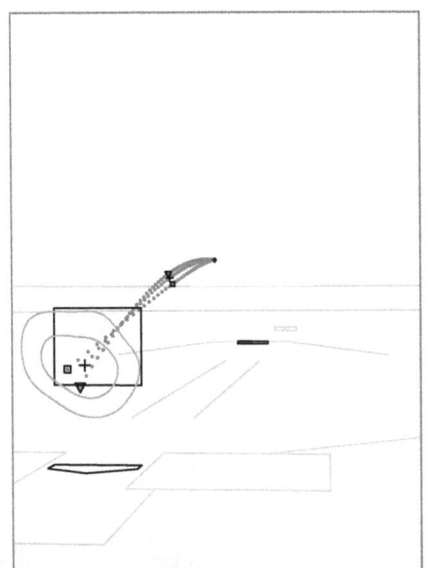

Pitch Shape vs RHH

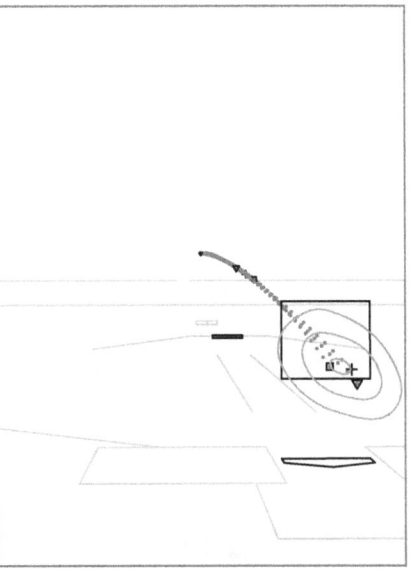

Type	Frequency	Velocity	H Movement	V Movement
● Fastball				
☐ Sinker	44.9%	92.9 [101]	-13.5 [95]	-20.1 [101]
+ Cutter	31.0%	87.9 [95]	5.4 [121]	-24.6 [98]
▲ Changeup				
✕ Splitter				
▽ Slider	21.5%	80.5 [83]	14.3 [139]	-35.5 [93]
◇ Curveball				
⬢ Slow Curveball				
✳ Knuckleball				
▼ Screwball				

Cole Hamels LHP

Born: 12/27/83 Age: 36 Bats: L Throws: L
Height: 6'4" Weight: 205 Origin: Round 1, 2002 Draft (#17 overall)

YEAR	TEAM	LVL	AGE	W	L	SV	G	GS	IP	H	HR	BB/9	K/9	K	GB%	BABIP
2017	FRI	AA	33	1	0	0	2	2	8^2	3	1	2.1	8.3	8	50%	.105
2017	TEX	MLB	33	11	6	0	24	24	148	125	18	3.2	6.4	105	48%	.251
2018	TEX	MLB	34	5	9	0	20	20	114^1	115	23	3.3	9.0	114	45%	.296
2018	CHN	MLB	34	4	3	0	12	12	76^1	61	6	2.7	8.7	74	49%	.286
2019	CHN	MLB	35	7	7	0	27	27	141^2	141	17	3.6	9.1	143	47%	.316
2020	ATL	MLB	36	10	9	0	28	28	157	154	24	3.4	9.1	158	46%	.302

Comparables: David Price, Mickey Lolich, Jon Lester

Hamels had an up-and-down '19. He was in the midst of a high-quality run when he injured his oblique in June. Upon returning, he just never seemed right. After signing with the Braves, Hamels conceded he came back too soon. Obviously the days of Hamels being considered an ace are far in the past, but he probably still has enough left in the tank to serve as a mid-rotation to back-end type. With a strong final act, he might even be able to pitch himself into Hall of Fame consideration. We'll save that conversation for another year.

YEAR	TEAM	LVL	AGE	WHIP	ERA	DRA	WARP	MPH	FB%	WHF	CSP
2017	FRI	AA	33	0.58	1.04	2.44	0.3				
2017	TEX	MLB	33	1.20	4.20	5.41	0.3	93.8	66.4	10	45.7
2018	TEX	MLB	34	1.37	4.72	5.17	0.2	93.7	67.8	13	45.7
2018	CHN	MLB	34	1.10	2.36	3.46	1.6	94.6	67.8	12.6	46.3
2019	CHN	MLB	35	1.39	3.81	4.87	1.4	93.3	66.3	12.9	47.6
2020	ATL	MLB	36	1.36	4.39	4.48	2.3	92.4	65.5	12	45.6

Cole Hamels, continued

Pitch Shape vs LHH

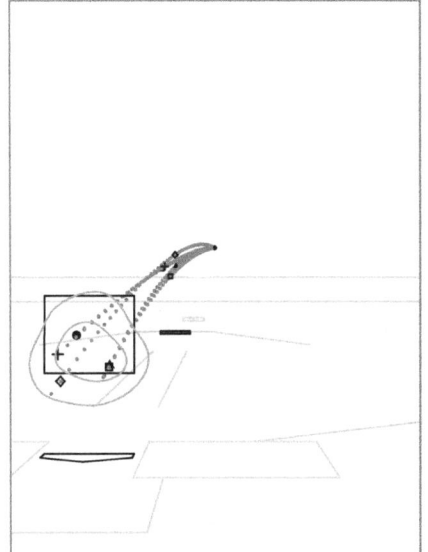

Pitch Shape vs RHH

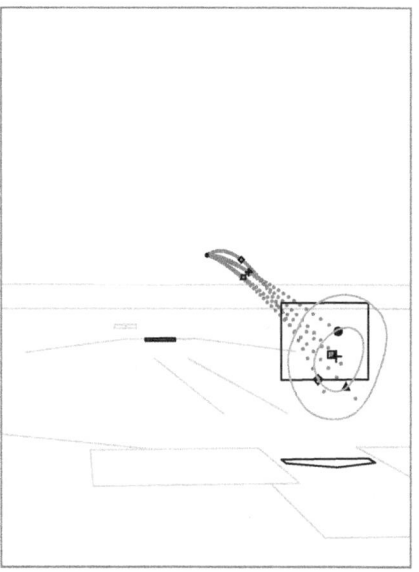

Type	Frequency	Velocity	H Movement	V Movement
● Fastball	35.3%	91.8 [98]	7.3 [98]	-15.1 [102]
☐ Sinker	12.3%	91.4 [94]	12.3 [103]	-20 [101]
+ Cutter	18.7%	88 [96]	0.4 [87]	-23.5 [102]
▲ Changeup	21.2%	83.6 [94]	12.1 [96]	-27.4 [100]
✕ Splitter				
▽ Slider				
◇ Curveball	12.4%	78.3 [99]	-4.8 [89]	-49.2 [97]
✦ Slow Curveball				
✱ Knuckleball				
▼ Screwball				

Félix Hernández RHP

Born: 04/08/86 Age: 34 Bats: R Throws: R
Height: 6'3" Weight: 225 Origin: International Free Agent, 2002

YEAR	TEAM	LVL	AGE	W	L	SV	G	GS	IP	H	HR	BB/9	K/9	K	GB%	BABIP
2017	TAC	AAA	31	2	0	0	3	3	13	9	1	2.1	11.1	16	42%	.267
2017	SEA	MLB	31	6	5	0	16	16	86^2	86	17	2.7	8.1	78	49%	.287
2018	SEA	MLB	32	8	14	0	29	28	155^2	159	27	3.4	7.2	125	48%	.286
2019	SEA	MLB	33	1	8	0	15	15	71^2	85	17	3.1	7.2	57	49%	.309
2020	SEA	MLB	34	2	2	0	33	0	35	38	7	3.1	7.8	30	48%	.301

Comparables: Dwight Gooden, Bert Blyleven, Matt Cain

"How many times do you think you cried tonight?" is not a question you'll hear often at a postgame press conference, but it was perfectly appropriate in the context: to Hernández, seated at the podium following his final start as a Mariner, smiling, but visibly drained. After mentioning a moment with his brother, Hernández paused in contemplation of the whole evening, before continuing: "It was fun!" On a night where a franchise said goodbye to its most loyal superstar, a borderline heartbreaking ending to wholly unfulfilled story, there was more than enough to be sad about. A team that had experienced strict disappointment over the King's 15-year tenure now had no choice but to let him go. And yet, here he was, beaming through the tears, proclaiming how much fun he had in his final, fitting act—a Mariners' defeat.

That, in many ways, was the beauty of Félix Hernández, Seattle Mariner. He was having fun when he was a 19-year-old baby-faced phenom. He was having fun at the peak of his powers, arguably the best pitcher on Earth. And he was still having fun at the end, a shell of the pitcher he once was. If Félix was having fun, we were having fun. He was as close to a one-man show as baseball can get, making every fifth day an event for a fan base that rarely had reason to care during the other four. Many pitied him. They couldn't fathom the endurance required to man the bilge pumps on a sinking ship. But he just wanted to perform his craft for the people that cheered him for his entire adult life. No matter the standings, no matter the score. That remained true all the way to the bitter end.

Hernández is 33 with an arm going on 40. It's possible he'll find a soft landing with a bad team in search of innings. Maybe he'll find somewhere else to have fun on a mound. But for now, Félix will move on, and the Mariners will march on without him, both still in search of October baseball. The drought is alive, but The King is dead. Long Live The King.

YEAR	TEAM	LVL	AGE	WHIP	ERA	DRA	WARP	MPH	FB%	WHF	CSP
2017	TAC	AAA	31	0.92	4.15	2.32	0.5				
2017	SEA	MLB	31	1.29	4.36	5.72	-0.1	92.5	44.5	10.2	46.5
2018	SEA	MLB	32	1.40	5.55	5.30	0.0	91.6	43.3	8.8	45.3
2019	SEA	MLB	33	1.53	6.40	7.10	-1.0	91.8	39.7	9.4	49.6
2020	SEA	MLB	34	1.42	5.40	5.29	0.0	90.7	41.8	9.1	46.7

Atlanta Braves 2020

Félix Hernández, continued

Pitch Shape vs LHH

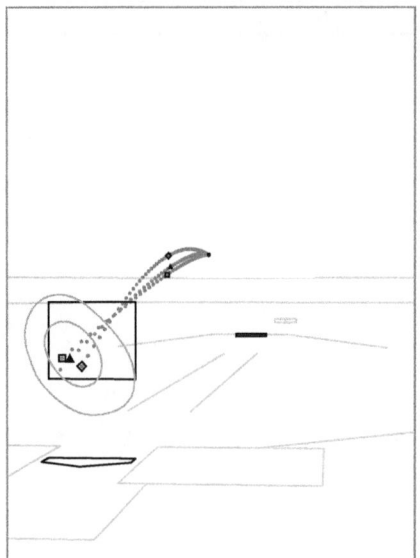

Pitch Shape vs RHH

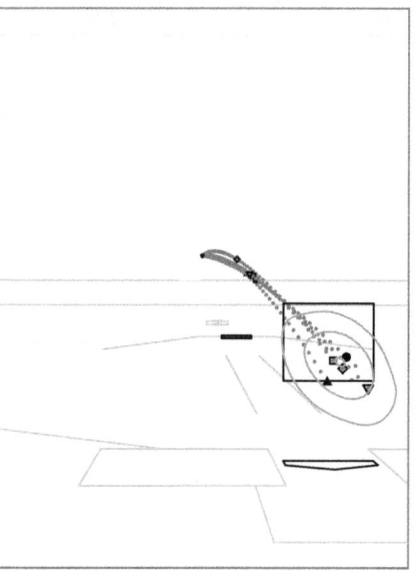

Type	Frequency	Velocity	H Movement	V Movement
● Fastball	8.1%	90.5 [95]	-4.5 [111]	-18 [95]
☐ Sinker	31.2%	89.9 [86]	-11.9 [105]	-22.8 [91]
+ Cutter				
▲ Changeup	16.4%	85.1 [100]	-8.6 [112]	-32.7 [85]
✕ Splitter				
▽ Slider	8.7%	84.1 [99]	3.9 [96]	-33.1 [100]
◇ Curveball	35.3%	79.8 [104]	9 [106]	-46.2 [103]
✦ Slow Curveball				
✱ Knuckleball				
▼ Screwball				

Luke Jackson RHP

Born: 08/24/91 Age: 28 Bats: R Throws: R
Height: 6'2" Weight: 210 Origin: Round 1, 2010 Draft (#45 overall)

YEAR	TEAM	LVL	AGE	W	L	SV	G	GS	IP	H	HR	BB/9	K/9	K	GB%	BABIP
2017	GWN	AAA	25	0	3	1	9	4	24^1	26	2	5.9	8.5	23	34%	.338
2017	ATL	MLB	25	2	0	0	43	0	50^2	55	4	3.4	5.9	33	43%	.311
2018	GWN	AAA	26	2	1	0	10	1	21^1	11	0	4.2	14.3	34	45%	.289
2018	ATL	MLB	26	1	2	1	35	0	40^2	41	3	4.6	10.2	46	50%	.339
2019	ATL	MLB	27	9	2	18	70	0	72^2	76	10	3.2	13.1	106	60%	.386
2020	ATL	MLB	28	2	2	0	43	0	45	43	5	4.1	12.0	60	53%	.346

Comparables: Jeremy Jeffress, Fernando Nieve, Nate Adcock

Following the 2018 season, all hope seemed to be lost for the unassuming reliever after two seasons in Atlanta. Jackson was destined to float through life in the major leagues as a hard-tosser who could never quite reach the level of reliability. Then on one fateful day between October 2018 and March 2019, Luke felt the bite of a radioactive slider. From that day forward, his life changed forever and he became your friendly neighborhood Slider-Man. With great power came great (high-leverage) responsibility. Jackson's slider—which he threw over 53 percent of the time—propelled him into the closer role for the Braves, but a tough July when he was done in by an unlikely foe saw him slide into middle relief. That unlikely foe? Right-handed hitters who patiently waded through breakers to tee off on his fastball. As the Braves continue to infuse talent into their bullpen, Jackson will have plenty of help in keeping foes off the basepaths at SunTrust Park and far from home.

YEAR	TEAM	LVL	AGE	WHIP	ERA	DRA	WARP	MPH	FB%	WHF	CSP
2017	GWN	AAA	25	1.73	6.29	6.72	-0.3				
2017	ATL	MLB	25	1.46	4.62	5.36	-0.1	96.8	51.1	11.5	43
2018	GWN	AAA	26	0.98	1.69	2.42	0.7				
2018	ATL	MLB	26	1.52	4.43	5.79	-0.4	96.3	41.7	11.7	42.7
2019	ATL	MLB	27	1.40	3.84	3.21	1.7	97.5	37.9	18	42
2020	ATL	MLB	28	1.41	3.95	4.02	0.7	96.5	41.7	15.2	42.8

Atlanta Braves 2020

Luke Jackson, continued

Pitch Shape vs LHH   **Pitch Shape vs RHH**

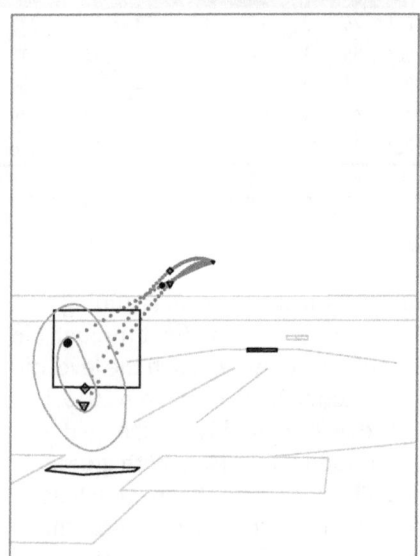 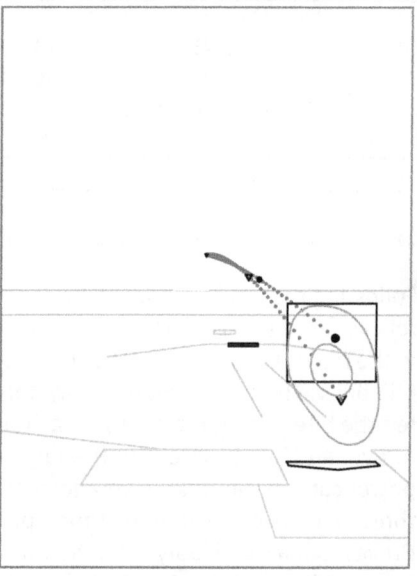

Type	Frequency	Velocity	H Movement	V Movement
● Fastball	37.9%	96.3 [111]	-6.2 [103]	-10.8 [113]
☐ Sinker				
+ Cutter				
▲ Changeup				
✕ Splitter				
▽ Slider	53.8%	87.8 [114]	2.3 [89]	-37.7 [87]
◇ Curveball	8.2%	84 [118]	6.8 [97]	-46.9 [101]
⬥ Slow Curveball				
✳ Knuckleball				
▼ Screwball				

Chris Martin RHP

Born: 06/02/86 Age: 34 Bats: R Throws: R
Height: 6'8" Weight: 215 Origin: Round 21, 2005 Draft (#627 overall)

YEAR	TEAM	LVL	AGE	W	L	SV	G	GS	IP	H	HR	BB/9	K/9	K	GB%	BABIP
2018	TEX	MLB	32	1	5	0	46	0	41²	46	5	1.1	8.0	37	41%	.323
2019	ATL	MLB	33	1	1	0	20	0	17²	17	1	0.5	11.2	22	52%	.356
2019	TEX	MLB	33	0	2	4	38	0	38	35	8	0.9	10.2	43	50%	.293
2020	ATL	MLB	34	2	2	0	43	0	45	45	6	2.0	9.6	49	49%	.315

Comparables: Rob Wooten, Casey Janssen, Chris Hatcher

After selling out shows across the world and taking a shine to Japan in particular, it's interesting to see Chris Martin eventually settle down and eventually enter the lane of Southern Relief Rock. After doing some shows across the Dallas-Fort Worth area for a little bit, he finally managed to pick up a residency gig in Atlanta where he could continue to play the hits. As a matter of fact, he had a show during this past September that could have been described as being "immaculate." The crowd was reportedly left speechless after Martin delivered nine consecutive classic tunes before making his exit. It was a quick performance, but it was all the people needed to remember the reason why Atlanta went out of their way to get him to perform in their city.

YEAR	TEAM	LVL	AGE	WHIP	ERA	DRA	WARP	MPH	FB%	WHF	CSP
2018	TEX	MLB	32	1.22	4.54	5.29	-0.2	97.0	72.4	10.1	50.9
2019	ATL	MLB	33	1.02	4.08	2.88	0.5	96.8	82.4	15.7	49.6
2019	TEX	MLB	33	1.03	3.08	3.22	0.9	97.7	82.4	13.6	54.8
2020	ATL	MLB	34	1.21	3.59	3.83	0.8	96.1	77.2	12.4	51.3

Atlanta Braves 2020

Chris Martin, continued

Pitch Shape vs LHH	Pitch Shape vs RHH
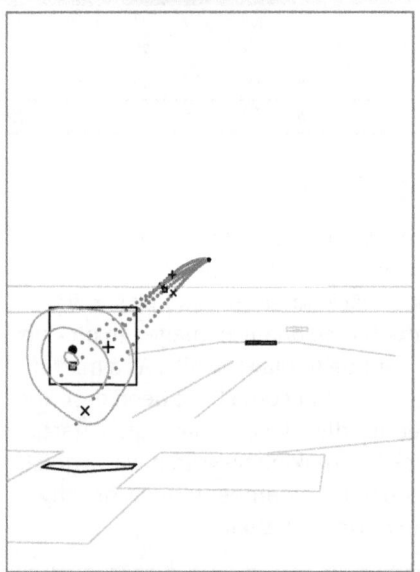	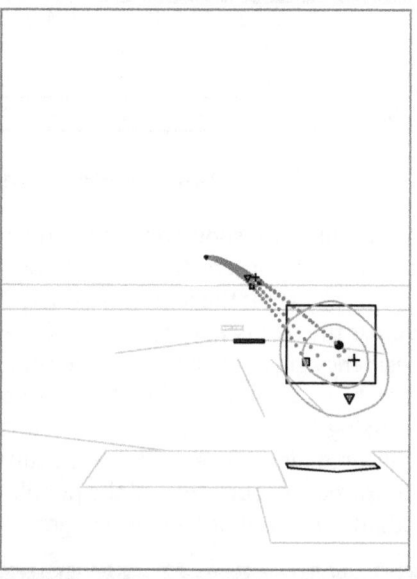

Type	Frequency	Velocity	H Movement	V Movement
● Fastball	46.9%	96.2 [111]	-6.1 [103]	-13 [108]
☐ Sinker	17.1%	95.6 [116]	-12.5 [101]	-16.7 [113]
+ Cutter	14.4%	91.8 [120]	3.1 [107]	-23.6 [102]
▲ Changeup				
✕ Splitter	12.2%	89.2 [118]	-9.8 [93]	-27.5 [106]
▽ Slider	9.4%	86.3 [108]	4.5 [98]	-34.6 [96]
◇ Curveball				
✦ Slow Curveball				
✳ Knuckleball				
▼ Screwball				

Mark Melancon RHP
Born: 03/28/85 Age: 35 Bats: R Throws: R
Height: 6'2" Weight: 215 Origin: Round 9, 2006 Draft (#284 overall)

YEAR	TEAM	LVL	AGE	W	L	SV	G	GS	IP	H	HR	BB/9	K/9	K	GB%	BABIP
2017	SFN	MLB	32	1	2	11	32	0	30	37	3	1.8	8.7	29	54%	.374
2018	SFN	MLB	33	1	4	3	41	0	39	48	2	3.2	7.2	31	52%	.365
2019	ATL	MLB	34	1	0	11	23	0	21	22	1	0.9	10.3	24	62%	.339
2019	SFN	MLB	34	4	2	1	43	0	46¹	49	3	3.1	8.5	44	60%	.354
2020	ATL	MLB	35	3	3	18	54	0	57	56	6	2.5	8.6	54	57%	.310

Comparables: Fernando Salas, Luke Gregerson, Mike Adams

While conventional reasoning would suggest that there are two sides to every story, there are three when it comes to Melancon: San Francisco's story, Atlanta's story, and the actual truth. If you hear it from Giants fans, you'll hear a cautionary tale of the dangers of being the team that decides to give an aging reliever such a hefty average annual value contract. If you hear it from Braves fans, you'll hear about Melancon being just what Atlanta needed to stabilize their bullpen—even if that comes with a $14 million price tag. The version of Melancon that showed up in Atlanta and recorded 11 saves with a resurgently low DRA was a throwback to the simpler days before the contract entered every conversation about the 34-year-old. In reality, the expensive truth lies somewhere in the middle, but as long as Melancon continues to rack up grounders and saves, the focus will be on his performance and not his salary.

YEAR	TEAM	LVL	AGE	WHIP	ERA	DRA	WARP	MPH	FB%	WHF	CSP
2017	SFN	MLB	32	1.43	4.50	2.75	0.8	93.5	74.7	10.6	43.9
2018	SFN	MLB	33	1.59	3.23	3.62	0.6	93.4	68.3	10.6	46.2
2019	ATL	MLB	34	1.14	3.86	2.21	0.7	93.6	68.8	12.6	44.2
2019	SFN	MLB	34	1.40	3.50	4.41	0.5	93.6	68.8	11.1	44.3
2020	ATL	MLB	35	1.27	3.59	3.77	1.0	92.3	68.3	11	44

Atlanta Braves 2020

Mark Melancon, continued

Pitch Shape vs LHH   Pitch Shape vs RHH

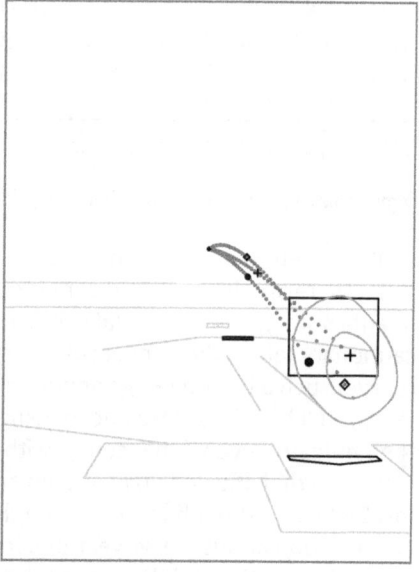

Type	Frequency	Velocity	H Movement	V Movement
● Fastball	4.8%	92.5 [100]	-6.4 [102]	-17.1 [97]
☐ Sinker				
+ Cutter	61.5%	92.1 [122]	1.2 [96]	-19.4 [117]
▲ Changeup				
✕ Splitter				
▽ Slider				
◇ Curveball	31.0%	82.3 [112]	3.8 [85]	-50.3 [94]
⊕ Slow Curveball				
✲ Knuckleball				
▼ Screwball				

A.J. Minter LHP

Born: 09/02/93 Age: 26 Bats: L Throws: L
Height: 6'0" Weight: 215 Origin: Round 2, 2015 Draft (#75 overall)

YEAR	TEAM	LVL	AGE	W	L	SV	G	GS	IP	H	HR	BB/9	K/9	K	GB%	BABIP
2017	GWN	AAA	23	1	2	0	17	0	15^1	15	1	5.9	10.0	17	30%	.326
2017	ATL	MLB	23	0	1	0	16	0	15	13	1	1.2	15.6	26	34%	.387
2018	ATL	MLB	24	4	3	15	65	0	61^1	57	3	3.2	10.1	69	39%	.329
2019	GWN	AAA	25	2	2	5	20	0	22^2	24	4	1.2	11.9	30	38%	.351
2019	ATL	MLB	25	3	4	5	36	0	29^1	36	3	7.1	10.7	35	40%	.388
2020	ATL	MLB	26	1	1	0	21	0	23	19	3	3.6	10.2	26	39%	.284

Comparables: Paul Fry, Steven Okert, Hung-Chih Kuo

Part of the chorus to the album-ending breakup tune "Stay Together" by The Neptunes has Pharrell crooning out "Never dreamt I'd speak the phrase, now what the [bleep] just happened?" That's the question a lot of Braves fans were asking with Minter during the 2019 season. How in the world did it come to this? How did a reliever who was being hailed as a mini-Craig Kimbrel go from pitching high-leverage innings one season to completely falling off a cliff and spending significant time in Triple-A the following season? A minor car accident in spring training started the year off on uneasy footing, but it was his fastball command that let him down in the end. He not only had trouble throwing strikes with it—leading to a walk rate more than double his 2018 figure—but even when he threw it for strikes, it found too much of the zone and too many barrels because of that. His .692 slugging percentage allowed on fastballs was almost twice as high as it was the year prior. Sometimes it's difficult to explain how that command dies out. This isn't to assume that all is lost for Minter, but he's going to have to figure out "what the [bleep] just happened" if he wants to pitch in high-leverage situations again.

YEAR	TEAM	LVL	AGE	WHIP	ERA	DRA	WARP	MPH	FB%	WHF	CSP
2017	GWN	AAA	23	1.63	4.70	6.10	-0.1				
2017	ATL	MLB	23	1.00	3.00	2.15	0.5	97.6	50.8	19.5	43
2018	ATL	MLB	24	1.29	3.23	3.42	1.1	98.7	49	15.8	48
2019	GWN	AAA	25	1.19	3.57	2.67	0.8				
2019	ATL	MLB	25	2.01	7.06	5.95	-0.2	97.6	39.3	15.3	45.3
2020	ATL	MLB	26	1.24	3.42	3.62	0.4	97.8	46.4	16.3	46.4

Atlanta Braves 2020

A.J. Minter, continued

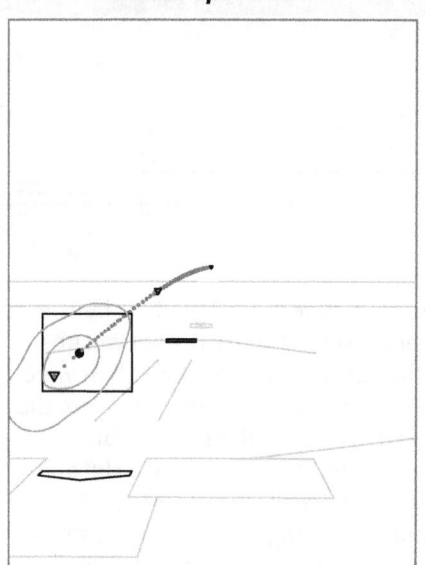
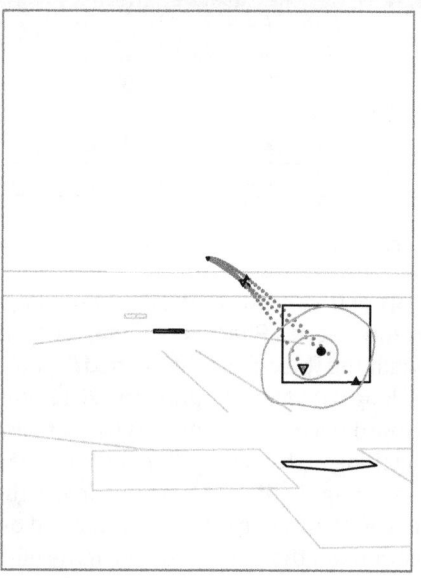

Type	Frequency	Velocity	H Movement	V Movement
● Fastball	39.3%	96.1 [110]	6.3 [103]	-12 [110]
☐ Sinker				
+ Cutter				
▲ Changeup	16.2%	86.2 [103]	12.7 [93]	-29.3 [95]
✕ Splitter				
▽ Slider	44.6%	91.6 [130]	-2.6 [90]	-21.7 [133]
◇ Curveball				
✧ Slow Curveball				
✱ Knuckleball				
▼ Screwball				

Sean Newcomb LHP

Born: 06/12/93   Age: 27   Bats: L   Throws: L
Height: 6'5"   Weight: 255   Origin: Round 1, 2014 Draft (#15 overall)

YEAR	TEAM	LVL	AGE	W	L	SV	G	GS	IP	H	HR	BB/9	K/9	K	GB%	BABIP
2017	GWN	AAA	24	3	3	0	11	11	57^2	45	3	5.2	11.5	74	41%	.304
2017	ATL	MLB	24	4	9	0	19	19	100	100	10	5.1	9.7	108	46%	.327
2018	ATL	MLB	25	12	9	0	31	30	164	137	18	4.4	8.8	160	44%	.273
2019	GWN	AAA	26	2	1	0	4	3	20^2	14	1	2.2	8.7	20	47%	.241
2019	ATL	MLB	26	6	3	1	55	4	68^1	61	8	3.8	8.6	65	50%	.282
2020	ATL	MLB	27	5	5	0	38	11	85	79	11	4.1	9.0	85	46%	.292

Comparables: Nick Pivetta, Cody Reed, Jordan Montgomery

On August 10, Newcomb faced two batters with the game tied in the tenth inning after the Braves blew a 6-2 lead against the Marlins in the bottom of the ninth. Newcomb proceeded to lose the game after allowing a hit, committing a throwing error and giving up a sacrifice fly in what felt like the blink of an eye. In his postgame rage, Newcomb kicked a trash can into a fire extinguisher. The fire extinguisher exploded and covered the entire visitors locker room with powder. If you're expecting this to be some sort of story that ends with Newcomb and the Braves going on a tear from that point forward, then you're in for a swerve. While Atlanta went 28-15 from that point on and comfortably clinched the division, Newcomb continued to blend in with the rest of the Braves bullpen. It's a far cry from where he started the season—as a burgeoning member of a young starting rotation—to a faceless member of the relief corps. The good news is that the hard-throwing left-hander has no discernible splits so he can be brought in to extinguish any kind of fire.

YEAR	TEAM	LVL	AGE	WHIP	ERA	DRA	WARP	MPH	FB%	WHF	CSP
2017	GWN	AAA	24	1.35	2.97	3.62	1.3				
2017	ATL	MLB	24	1.57	4.32	4.61	1.1	96.8	63.4	12.7	42.8
2018	ATL	MLB	25	1.33	3.90	3.83	2.8	95.8	62.4	11	46.3
2019	GWN	AAA	26	0.92	2.18	2.22	0.9				
2019	ATL	MLB	26	1.32	3.16	4.13	1.0	96.8	65.2	10.4	48.8
2020	ATL	MLB	27	1.38	4.08	4.19	1.4	95.8	64.1	11.4	47

Atlanta Braves 2020

Sean Newcomb, continued

Pitch Shape vs LHH

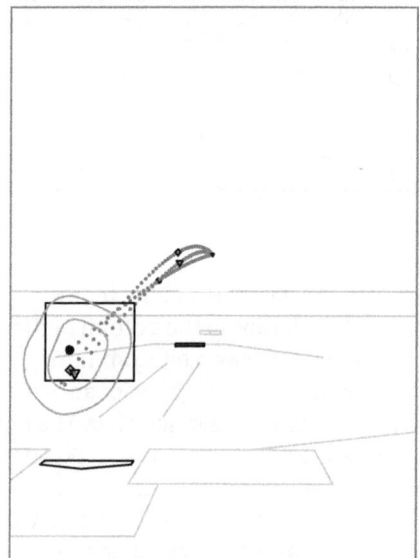

Pitch Shape vs RHH

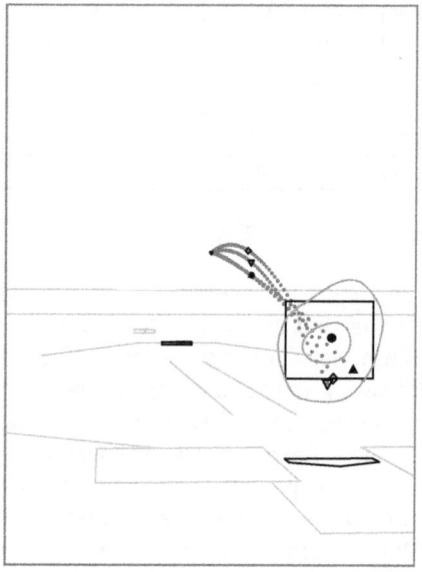

Type	Frequency	Velocity	H Movement	V Movement
● Fastball	65.2%	94.4 [106]	5 [108]	-12.7 [109]
☐ Sinker				
+ Cutter				
▲ Changeup	6.9%	87.4 [108]	11.1 [100]	-24.4 [109]
✕ Splitter				
▽ Slider	8.6%	81.3 [87]	-11.4 [127]	-43.6 [70]
◇ Curveball	19.3%	78.8 [101]	-7.2 [99]	-56.2 [82]
⊕ Slow Curveball				
✳ Knuckleball				
▼ Screwball				

Will Smith LHP

Born: 07/10/89   Age: 30   Bats: R   Throws: L
Height: 6'5"   Weight: 248   Origin: Round 7, 2008 Draft (#229 overall)

YEAR	TEAM	LVL	AGE	W	L	SV	G	GS	IP	H	HR	BB/9	K/9	K	GB%	BABIP
2018	SFN	MLB	28	2	3	14	54	0	53	37	3	2.5	12.1	71	41%	.281
2019	SFN	MLB	29	6	0	34	63	0	65[1]	46	10	2.9	13.2	96	44%	.277
2020	ATL	MLB	30	3	2	16	54	0	57	45	7	3.2	12.8	81	42%	.307

Comparables: Jake McGee, Brad Hand, Rafael Soriano

This fall has been a big one for Will Smith vs. Will Smith confrontations. But where October's release of *Gemini Man* was forgettable, the September 5 game between the Dodgers and Giants had the Hollywood drama. The elder Will M. Smith faced off against Dodgers rookie catcher Will D. Smith. Naturally it had to be part of one of the game's fiercest rivalries, with everything boiling down to two outs, bottom of the ninth, just like a screenwriter would craft it.

The broad themes were there too: after all, the veteran southpaw reliever had just reached the promised peak of his career; ensconced as the team's closer and named to his first All-Star Game, the strikeout artist was in the middle of his best season. The tyro facing him had the advantages of youth, raw athleticism, and was playing for a superior Dodgers team—all the benefits of Junior over Henry Brogan—but the elder Smith set down the younger with a strikeout to end the game.

The curtains closed on the 2019 season, and the Giants reliever would be just slightly overtaken by his rookie counterpart, 1.9 WARP to his own 1.8. But that fraction is well within the error bars, and the All-Star appearance pushes favor to the veteran lefty, at least for this season. It's likely that this Will Smith will have to be every bit as good as he was last season in order to stave off his doppelgänger for one more year, lest he be resigned to the role of second-best player with his famous name.

YEAR	TEAM	LVL	AGE	WHIP	ERA	DRA	WARP	MPH	FB%	WHF	CSP
2018	SFN	MLB	28	0.98	2.55	3.34	1.0	94.8	46.1	15.8	50.7
2019	SFN	MLB	29	1.03	2.76	2.84	1.8	94.5	47	16.4	45.3
2020	ATL	MLB	30	1.15	2.86	3.14	1.4	93.9	46.5	16.1	47.6

Atlanta Braves 2020

Will Smith, continued

Pitch Shape vs LHH
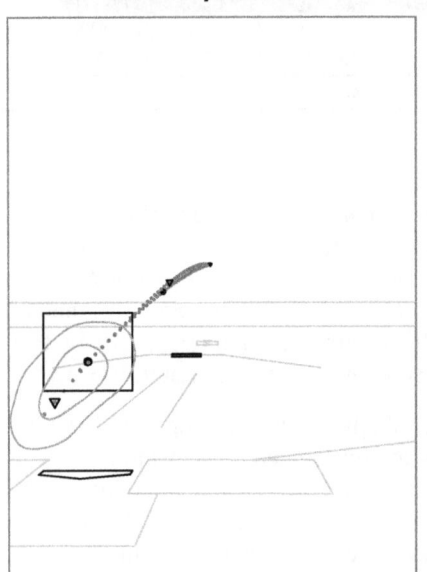

Pitch Shape vs RHH
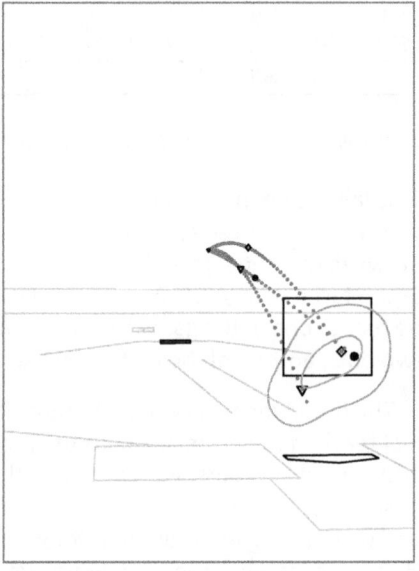

Type	Frequency	Velocity	H Movement	V Movement
● Fastball	47.0%	92.9 [101]	5.1 [108]	-13.3 [107]
□ Sinker				
+ Cutter				
▲ Changeup				
× Splitter				
▽ Slider	42.3%	81.8 [89]	-7.7 [111]	-35.9 [92]
◇ Curveball	8.9%	77.4 [96]	-7.2 [99]	-48.1 [99]
✦ Slow Curveball				
✱ Knuckleball				
▼ Screwball				

Mike Soroka   RHP
Born: 08/04/97   Age: 22   Bats: R   Throws: R
Height: 6'5"   Weight: 225   Origin: Round 1, 2015 Draft (#28 overall)

YEAR	TEAM	LVL	AGE	W	L	SV	G	GS	IP	H	HR	BB/9	K/9	K	GB%	BABIP
2017	MIS	AA	19	11	8	0	26	26	153^2	133	10	2.0	7.3	125	49%	.275
2018	GWN	AAA	20	2	1	0	5	5	27	20	0	2.0	10.3	31	70%	.299
2018	ATL	MLB	20	2	1	0	5	5	25^2	30	1	2.5	7.4	21	45%	.345
2019	GWN	AAA	21	1	0	0	2	2	9^1	5	1	1.0	9.6	10	73%	.190
2019	ATL	MLB	21	13	4	0	29	29	174^2	153	14	2.1	7.3	142	53%	.280
2020	ATL	MLB	22	11	9	0	29	29	172	174	20	2.6	7.7	147	53%	.303

Comparables: Jordan Lyles, Taijuan Walker, Tyler Skaggs

When you look at Soroka's body of work on paper, it's eye-popping. It's magisterial. It's truly a work of art. That is in stark contrast to what you see when he's pitching and he's on his A-game. Time seems to speed up and he lulls you into a false sense of complacency. He's not a boring pitcher, but he's not going to blow you away with his velocity or movement. Instead, he just spends his time casually painting the corners of the strike zone and inducing a pop fly every now and then until you look up and seven innings have passed in the blink of an eye. It's similar to how avid painters could lose an hour or two simply by watching Bob Ross calmly paint happy trees on a blank easel. Soroka has yet to paint a true masterpiece but if (and when) it happens, it'll happen before you realize what's really going on and you'll appreciate what he's done once he's finished.

YEAR	TEAM	LVL	AGE	WHIP	ERA	DRA	WARP	MPH	FB%	WHF	CSP
2017	MIS	AA	19	1.09	2.75	3.54	3.0				
2018	GWN	AAA	20	0.96	2.00	2.73	0.9				
2018	ATL	MLB	20	1.44	3.51	4.64	0.2	95.3	68.9	10.4	48.9
2019	GWN	AAA	21	0.64	3.86	2.20	0.4				
2019	ATL	MLB	21	1.11	2.68	3.24	4.8	94.7	63.3	10.9	47.8
2020	ATL	MLB	22	1.30	3.84	4.02	3.4	94.8	66.6	11.3	50.3

Atlanta Braves 2020

Mike Soroka, continued

Pitch Shape vs LHH

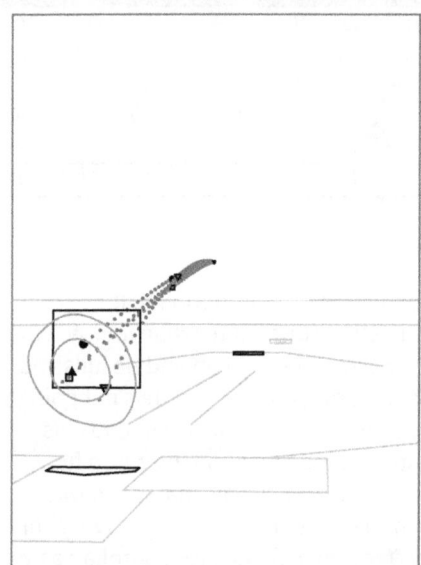

Pitch Shape vs RHH

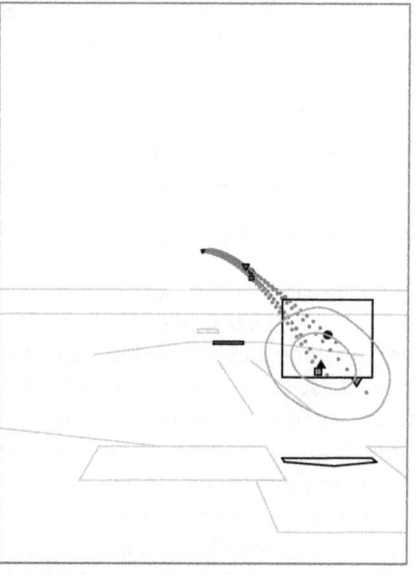

Type	Frequency	Velocity	H Movement	V Movement
● Fastball	18.4%	93 [102]	-4.2 [112]	-16.4 [99]
☐ Sinker	44.9%	92.3 [99]	-13.4 [95]	-21.9 [95]
+ Cutter				
▲ Changeup	12.4%	81.3 [86]	-11.7 [98]	-25.8 [105]
✕ Splitter				
▽ Slider	24.3%	83.2 [95]	5.5 [102]	-38.2 [85]
◇ Curveball				
✦ Slow Curveball				
✱ Knuckleball				
▼ Screwball				

Josh Tomlin RHP

Born: 10/19/84 Age: 35 Bats: R Throws: R
Height: 6'1" Weight: 190 Origin: Round 19, 2006 Draft (#581 overall)

YEAR	TEAM	LVL	AGE	W	L	SV	G	GS	IP	H	HR	BB/9	K/9	K	GB%	BABIP
2017	CLE	MLB	32	10	9	0	26	26	141	166	23	0.9	7.0	109	42%	.329
2018	COH	AAA	33	0	1	0	3	3	9^1	19	3	0.0	7.7	8	37%	.457
2018	CLE	MLB	33	2	5	0	32	9	70^1	92	25	1.5	5.9	46	32%	.286
2019	ATL	MLB	34	2	1	2	51	1	79^1	82	14	0.8	5.8	51	35%	.274
2020	ATL	MLB	35	2	2	0	33	0	35	42	10	1.6	6.2	24	36%	.295

Comparables: Tommy Hunter, Yohan Pino, Doug Fister

Going into the 2019 season, Tomlin had a clear reputation: He hated walks like your dog hated the vacuum cleaner. It seemed like he was pitching as if he was trying to avoid walking the batter at all costs. As it turned out, his walk-averse ways on the mound ended up transforming him from a waning starter to a somewhat reliable middle reliever. What's intriguing is that he managed to cut his home-run rate in half and did so without impeding on his strike-throwing proclivities. He's not someone you want for a high-leverage situation, but he's easy on the eyes and regardless of whether it works or not, you know it'll be over quickly.

YEAR	TEAM	LVL	AGE	WHIP	ERA	DRA	WARP	MPH	FB%	WHF	CSP
2017	CLE	MLB	32	1.28	4.98	4.44	1.8	89.4	71.8	9.6	49.1
2018	COH	AAA	33	2.04	6.75	8.32	-0.3				
2018	CLE	MLB	33	1.48	6.14	6.87	-1.4	89.8	72.7	9.4	49.9
2019	ATL	MLB	34	1.12	3.74	5.27	0.1	90.6	74.1	10.1	47.3
2020	ATL	MLB	35	1.39	5.77	5.98	-0.2	88.8	71.5	9.5	47.7

Atlanta Braves 2020

Josh Tomlin, continued

Pitch Shape vs LHH

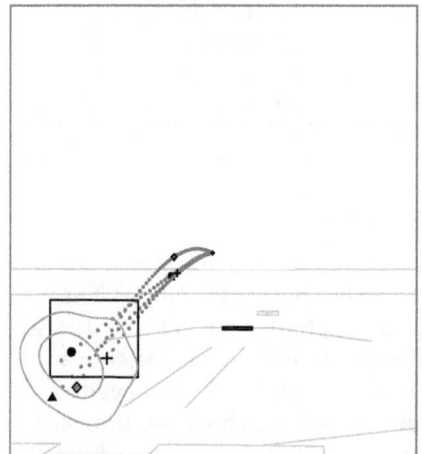

Pitch Shape vs RHH

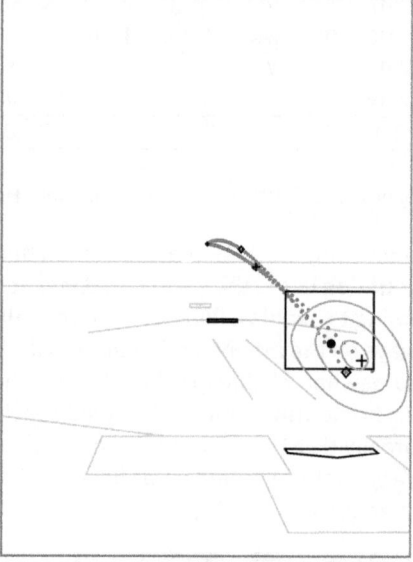

Touki Toussaint RHP
Born: 06/20/96   Age: 24   Bats: R   Throws: R
Height: 6'3"   Weight: 185   Origin: Round 1, 2014 Draft (#16 overall)

YEAR	TEAM	LVL	AGE	W	L	SV	G	GS	IP	H	HR	BB/9	K/9	K	GB%	BABIP
2017	BRV	A+	21	3	9	0	19	19	105^1	101	8	3.6	10.5	123	45%	.324
2017	MIS	AA	21	3	4	0	7	7	39^2	30	3	5.0	10.0	44	38%	.276
2018	MIS	AA	22	4	6	0	16	16	86	66	7	3.8	11.2	107	48%	.284
2018	GWN	AAA	22	5	0	0	8	8	50^1	35	0	3.0	10.0	56	44%	.280
2018	ATL	MLB	22	2	1	0	7	5	29	18	1	6.5	9.9	32	47%	.254
2019	GWN	AAA	23	1	6	0	10	10	39^2	51	5	6.4	10.0	44	43%	.393
2019	ATL	MLB	23	4	0	0	24	1	41^2	44	5	5.6	9.7	45	44%	.339
2020	ATL	MLB	24	4	4	0	20	10	60	56	8	4.8	9.5	63	43%	.301

Comparables: Sean Reid-Foley, Zack Littell, Jake Faria

It might sound absurd to say that a guy who's about to turn 24 is going into a make-or-break season, but that could indeed be the case for Toussaint in 2020. It's one thing to take a step back when it comes to making progress as a major leaguer, but it's a completely different thing to take a bit of a step back in Triple-A on top of that, as Touki didn't fare too much better while wearing a Stripers jersey. If and when the 2014 draft pick carves out a role in the majors, it's likely going to be in the bullpen, but he's going to need some semblance of control in order for his plus stuff to be useful in-game. That fearsome curveball still flashes under the surface and his split would be a weapon against lefties if he knew where it was going. Instead, left-handed batters waited on his fastball and tattooed him for a 1.205 OPS. On a team with less pitching depth, he'd have more opportunity to work through these issues, but that's not the situation at hand here.

YEAR	TEAM	LVL	AGE	WHIP	ERA	DRA	WARP	MPH	FB%	WHF	CSP
2017	BRV	A+	21	1.36	5.04	4.84	0.5				
2017	MIS	AA	21	1.31	3.18	4.37	0.4				
2018	MIS	AA	22	1.19	2.93	3.46	1.9				
2018	GWN	AAA	22	1.03	1.43	2.75	1.6				
2018	ATL	MLB	22	1.34	4.03	4.69	0.2	95.9	53.4	9.9	43.6
2019	GWN	AAA	23	1.99	7.49	6.83	0.0				
2019	ATL	MLB	23	1.68	5.62	4.80	0.3	95.8	49.2	12.4	41.2
2020	ATL	MLB	24	1.46	4.61	4.56	0.8	95.6	52.1	11.9	43.6

Atlanta Braves 2020

Touki Toussaint, continued

Pitch Shape vs LHH   **Pitch Shape vs RHH**

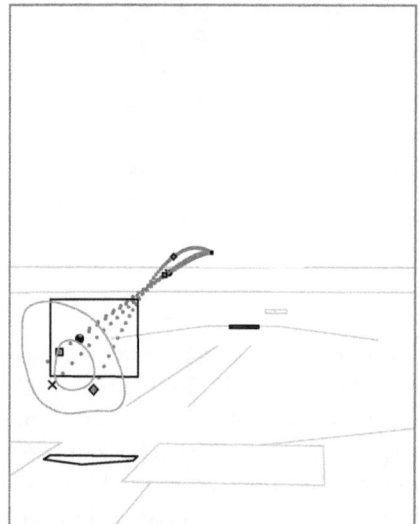
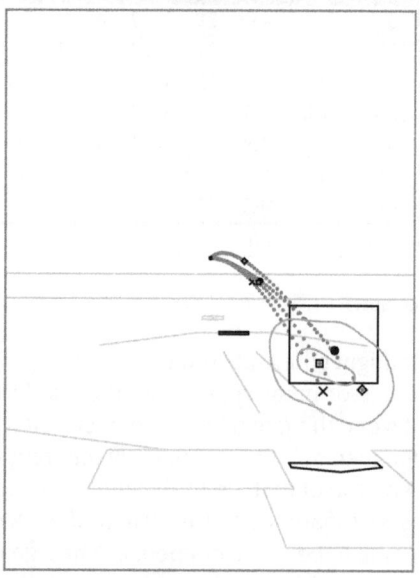

Type	Frequency	Velocity	H Movement	V Movement
● Fastball	22.7%	94 [105]	-7.3 [98]	-16.6 [98]
☐ Sinker	26.5%	93.5 [105]	-12.9 [98]	-21.7 [95]
+ Cutter				
▲ Changeup				
✕ Splitter	23.3%	86.6 [107]	-7.7 [101]	-31 [94]
▽ Slider				
◇ Curveball	27.5%	77.7 [97]	11.7 [117]	-51.9 [91]
⊕ Slow Curveball				
✳ Knuckleball				
▼ Screwball				

Jacob Webb RHP
Born: 08/15/93 Age: 26 Bats: R Throws: R
Height: 6'1" Weight: 200 Origin: Round 18, 2014 Draft (#553 overall)

YEAR	TEAM	LVL	AGE	W	L	SV	G	GS	IP	H	HR	BB/9	K/9	K	GB%	BABIP
2017	BRV	A+	23	2	1	2	22	0	41^{1}	29	1	4.8	10.5	48	43%	.289
2017	MIS	AA	23	3	1	0	16	0	24	17	1	5.2	9.8	26	36%	.276
2018	MIS	AA	24	1	2	7	21	0	22^{2}	16	4	4.8	13.9	35	45%	.255
2018	GWN	AAA	24	2	2	11	30	0	31^{2}	20	3	3.1	9.7	34	42%	.218
2019	GWN	AAA	25	0	1	1	10	0	10^{1}	9	1	7.8	10.5	12	50%	.296
2019	ATL	MLB	25	4	0	2	36	0	32^{1}	24	4	3.3	7.8	28	40%	.233
2020	ATL	MLB	26	1	1	0	21	0	23	21	4	4.2	9.1	23	40%	.290

Comparables: Mark Worrell, Ian Gibaut, Sam Tuivailala

As far as coverage of aspiring minor leaguers go, we're in a bit of a golden age. It's not particularly hard to find information on plenty of prospects, so there's less mystery and intrigue surrounding the arrival of young players in the major leagues. However, some guys can still fall through the cracks to make an anonymous arrival and Webb falls into that category. Even when he was actually showing up on prospect lists, he still elicited a reaction of "Who?" from casual fans when he made it to Atlanta. He continued to toil in obscurity while he racking up productive relief appearances for the Braves. An elbow impingement cut his season short, but it's clear that Webb does indeed have what it takes to stick around as a reliever at this level, even if his ERA overstates the impact.

YEAR	TEAM	LVL	AGE	WHIP	ERA	DRA	WARP	MPH	FB%	WHF	CSP
2017	BRV	A+	23	1.23	1.74	3.42	0.7				
2017	MIS	AA	23	1.29	2.62	4.15	0.2				
2018	MIS	AA	24	1.24	3.18	3.09	0.5				
2018	GWN	AAA	24	0.98	3.13	2.76	0.9				
2019	GWN	AAA	25	1.74	6.97	4.45	0.2				
2019	ATL	MLB	25	1.11	1.39	4.91	0.2	96.4	54.5	13.3	46.5
2020	ATL	MLB	26	1.40	4.38	4.48	0.2	96.0	55.5	13.5	47.3

Atlanta Braves 2020

Jacob Webb, continued

Pitch Shape vs LHH

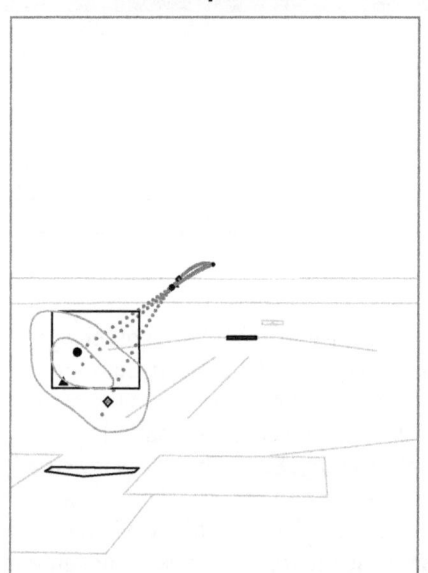

Pitch Shape vs RHH

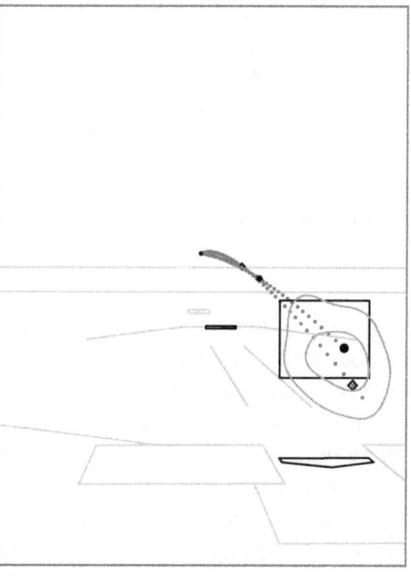

Type	Frequency	Velocity	H Movement	V Movement
● Fastball	54.5%	95.2 [108]	-10.9 [82]	-13 [108]
☐ Sinker				
+ Cutter				
▲ Changeup	12.4%	85.8 [102]	-15.9 [78]	-25.5 [106]
✕ Splitter				
▽ Slider				
◇ Curveball	33.1%	81.6 [110]	6.3 [95]	-41 [114]
✦ Slow Curveball				
✱ Knuckleball				
▼ Screwball				

Bryse Wilson   RHP

Born: 12/20/97   Age: 22   Bats: R   Throws: R
Height: 6'1"   Weight: 225   Origin: Round 4, 2016 Draft (#109 overall)

YEAR	TEAM	LVL	AGE	W	L	SV	G	GS	IP	H	HR	BB/9	K/9	K	GB%	BABIP
2017	ROM	A	19	10	7	0	26	26	137	105	8	2.4	9.1	139	54%	.272
2018	BRV	A+	20	2	0	0	5	5	26^2	16	0	2.4	8.8	26	60%	.229
2018	MIS	AA	20	3	5	0	15	15	77	77	3	3.0	10.4	89	44%	.347
2018	GWN	AAA	20	3	0	0	5	3	22	20	6	1.2	11.5	28	45%	.280
2018	ATL	MLB	20	1	0	0	3	1	7	8	0	7.7	7.7	6	29%	.381
2019	GWN	AAA	21	10	7	0	21	21	121	120	12	1.9	8.8	118	46%	.316
2019	ATL	MLB	21	1	1	0	6	4	20	26	5	4.5	7.2	16	34%	.339
2020	ATL	MLB	22	3	3	0	37	5	58	60	10	2.9	7.9	51	40%	.294

Comparables: Lucas Giolito, Jaime Barria, Jake Thompson

Wilson ended up starting the 2019 season with the Braves, but it was pretty evident by his subsequent cameo appearances across the rest of the season that he was not ready for the majors. The good news is that the Braves weren't counting on him being ready and are continuing to be patient with the 22-year-old. While the new balls were flying all over the International League, Wilson did a great job of keeping the ball in the yard and limiting unnecessary baserunners by posting the best walk rate of his pro career. And despite a step back in his strikeout rate, it allowed him to pitch deeper into games as he made it through at least six innings in 13 of his 21 starts, including his final eight in a row in Gwinnett. Wilson is going to get plenty of time to figure out whether his future is in the rotation.

YEAR	TEAM	LVL	AGE	WHIP	ERA	DRA	WARP	MPH	FB%	WHF	CSP
2017	ROM	A	19	1.04	2.50	3.33	3.1				
2018	BRV	A+	20	0.86	0.34	2.48	0.9				
2018	MIS	AA	20	1.34	3.97	4.63	0.6				
2018	GWN	AAA	20	1.05	5.32	3.38	0.5				
2018	ATL	MLB	20	2.00	6.43	5.37	0.0	97.0	71.1	15.6	45.4
2019	GWN	AAA	21	1.21	3.42	3.27	4.0				
2019	ATL	MLB	21	1.80	7.20	7.30	-0.3	96.6	71.9	9.5	47.6
2020	ATL	MLB	22	1.35	4.61	4.77	0.5	96.7	74.7	11.4	48.6

Atlanta Braves 2020

Bryse Wilson, continued

Pitch Shape vs LHH	Pitch Shape vs RHH
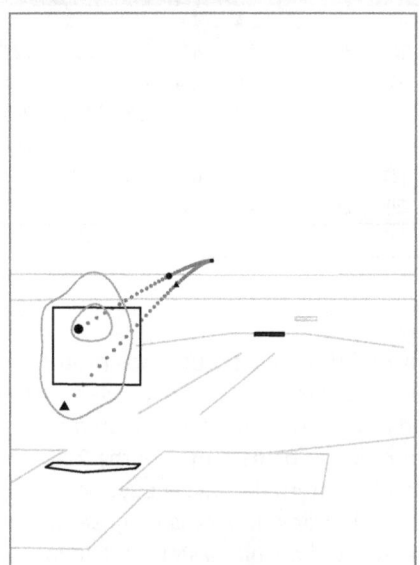	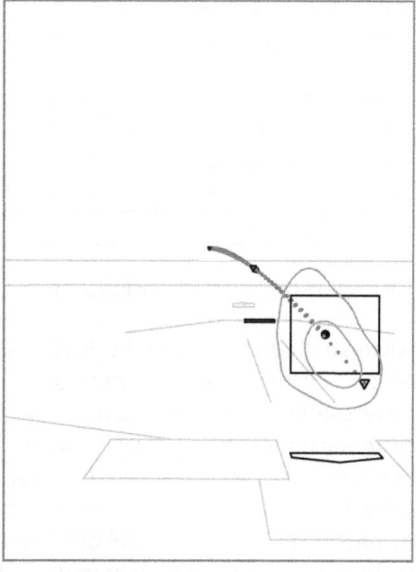

Type	Frequency	Velocity	H Movement	V Movement
● Fastball	66.6%	94.8 [107]	-7.6 [97]	-14.1 [105]
☐ Sinker	5.3%	92.9 [101]	-13.9 [92]	-22 [94]
+ Cutter				
▲ Changeup	13.5%	85 [99]	-13.5 [89]	-30.2 [92]
✕ Splitter				
▽ Slider	12.4%	83.9 [98]	5.6 [103]	-32.9 [100]
◇ Curveball				
⊕ Slow Curveball				
✱ Knuckleball				
▼ Screwball				

Kyle Wright RHP

Born: 10/02/95 Age: 24 Bats: R Throws: R
Height: 6'4" Weight: 200 Origin: Round 1, 2017 Draft (#5 overall)

YEAR	TEAM	LVL	AGE	W	L	SV	G	GS	IP	H	HR	BB/9	K/9	K	GB%	BABIP
2017	BRV	A+	21	0	1	0	6	6	11^1	8	0	3.2	7.9	10	61%	.258
2018	MIS	AA	22	6	8	0	20	20	109^1	103	6	3.5	8.6	105	56%	.311
2018	GWN	AAA	22	2	1	0	7	4	28^2	15	2	2.5	8.8	28	51%	.183
2018	ATL	MLB	22	0	0	0	4	0	6	4	2	9.0	7.5	5	41%	.133
2019	GWN	AAA	23	11	4	0	21	21	112^1	107	13	2.8	9.3	116	48%	.313
2019	ATL	MLB	23	0	3	0	7	4	19^2	24	4	5.9	8.2	18	43%	.351
2020	ATL	MLB	24	4	5	0	37	10	78	83	12	3.7	7.8	68	47%	.308

Comparables: Reynaldo López, Zack Wheeler, Zack Littell

For a prospect who ended up making the Opening Day roster for a playoff contender, there weren't really too many accompanying expectations for Wright in 2019. If anything, he just happened to be in the right place at the right time during the first week of the season. This was more of a learning year for Wright than anything else with two of the most common issues to tackle among upper-level prospects: fastball command and some sort of reliable third pitch to go with his mid-90s fastball and hard slider. He simplified his approach tremendously when he made a few relief appearances in September and looked excellent while doing so. While having their second-highest draft pick of the century turn out to be a potential impact reliever isn't the outcome the Braves were hoping for, that may just be what they get in the former Vanderbilt ace if Wright can't solve at least one of those two lingering issues.

YEAR	TEAM	LVL	AGE	WHIP	ERA	DRA	WARP	MPH	FB%	WHF	CSP
2017	BRV	A+	21	1.06	3.18	3.01	0.3				
2018	MIS	AA	22	1.34	3.70	4.12	1.6				
2018	GWN	AAA	22	0.80	2.51	2.15	1.1				
2018	ATL	MLB	22	1.67	4.50	4.98	0.0	95.8	51.6	10.2	37.6
2019	GWN	AAA	23	1.26	4.17	3.54	3.4				
2019	ATL	MLB	23	1.88	8.69	6.33	-0.1	96.6	54.4	9.7	42.6
2020	ATL	MLB	24	1.48	5.10	5.06	0.5	96.3	55.4	10.1	41.6

Atlanta Braves 2020

Kyle Wright, continued

Pitch Shape vs LHH

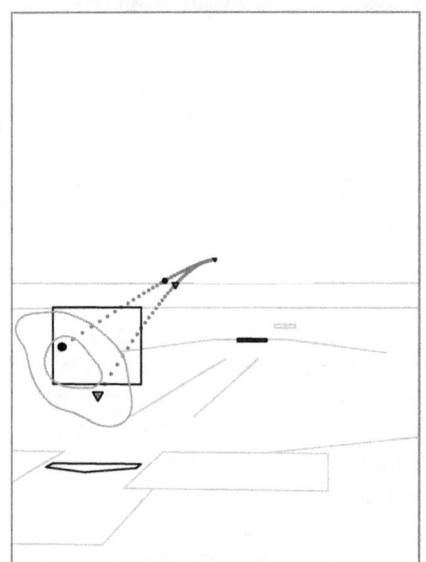

Pitch Shape vs RHH

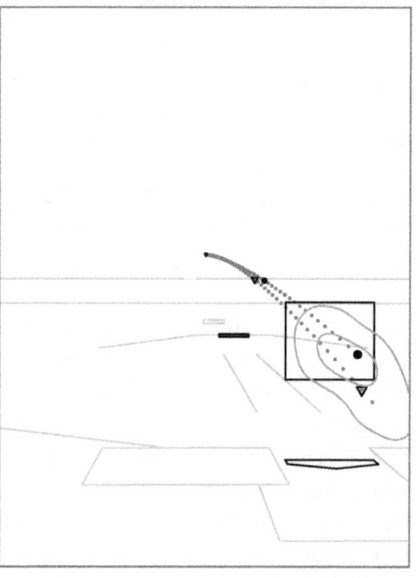

Type	Frequency	Velocity	H Movement	V Movement
● Fastball	43.3%	94.9 [107]	-6.2 [103]	-14.7 [103]
☐ Sinker	11.1%	94 [107]	-11.9 [105]	-21.4 [97]
+ Cutter				
▲ Changeup	7.7%	86 [103]	-12.5 [94]	-25.6 [105]
✕ Splitter				
▽ Slider	25.9%	87.2 [112]	3.3 [93]	-29.7 [110]
◇ Curveball	12.0%	80.7 [107]	14 [126]	-42.1 [112]
✦ Slow Curveball				
✳ Knuckleball				
▼ Screwball				

PLAYER COMMENTS WITHOUT GRAPHS

Ronald Acuña Jr. OF
Born: 12/18/97   Age: 22   Bats: R   Throws: R
Height: 6'0"   Weight: 180   Origin: International Free Agent, 2014

YEAR	TEAM	LVL	AGE	PA	R	2B	3B	HR	RBI	BB	K	SB	CS	AVG/OBP/SLG
2017	BRV	A+	19	126	21	3	5	3	19	8	40	14	3	.287/.336/.478
2017	MIS	AA	19	243	29	14	1	9	30	18	56	19	11	.326/.374/.520
2017	GWN	AAA	19	243	38	14	2	9	33	17	48	11	6	.344/.393/.548
2018	GWN	AAA	20	101	9	2	0	1	3	11	25	5	1	.211/.297/.267
2018	ATL	MLB	20	487	78	26	4	26	64	45	123	16	5	.293/.366/.552
2019	ATL	MLB	21	715	127	22	2	41	101	76	188	37	9	.280/.365/.518
2020	ATL	MLB	22	595	84	27	3	31	92	54	155	23	9	.283/.355/.519

Comparables: Mike Trout, Ozzie Albies, Bryce Harper

Roles play an extremely important part in the success of any group effort, and especially so in baseball. Just because someone has the skills for one role doesn't mean that it's the best one for them or for the group as a whole. In the case of Acuña, he started out the 2019 season as a cleanup hitter since he led the Braves in home runs during 2018. While Acuña is a dynamic enough talent to succeed in that role, the team wasn't playing at the same level as before. On May 10, Acuña was put back in the leadoff spot. By June 10, the Braves were at the top of their division and never looked back.

Acuña serves as a tone-setter. He is the straw that stirs the drink. He is the drummer who brings rhythm to the rest of the lineup. He's just as electrifying on defense as he is on offense, and serious flirtation with a 40/40 season goes a long way towards showing what the young Venezuelan is like at the plate and on the basepaths. Atlanta has a superstar talent on their hands, and Acuña is now very comfortable in his role at the top of the lineup.

YEAR	TEAM	LVL	AGE	PA	DRC+	VORP	BABIP	BRR	FRAA	WARP
2017	BRV	A+	19	126	111	7.7	.411	1.2	CF(19): -1.8, RF(9): 0.1	0.4
2017	MIS	AA	19	243	153	21.0	.396	0.6	CF(34): -1.0, RF(14): -1.4	1.8
2017	GWN	AAA	19	243	161	17.1	.404	0.0	CF(20): 1.7, RF(20): 2.8	2.5
2018	GWN	AAA	20	101	74	-2.2	.281	1.0	LF(18): -3.1, CF(2): -0.6	-0.3
2018	ATL	MLB	20	487	137	48.6	.352	3.1	LF(101): -10.8, CF(13): 1.0	2.9
2019	ATL	MLB	21	715	129	51.1	.337	8.6	CF(100): -3.2, LF(46): 5.0	6.1
2020	ATL	MLB	22	595	125	37.9	.343	3.4	RF -2, CF -1	3.5

William Contreras C

Born: 12/24/97 Age: 22 Bats: R Throws: R
Height: 6'0" Weight: 180 Origin: International Free Agent, 2015

YEAR	TEAM	LVL	AGE	PA	R	2B	3B	HR	RBI	BB	K	SB	CS	AVG/OBP/SLG
2017	DNV	RK	19	198	29	10	1	4	25	24	30	1	0	.290/.379/.432
2018	ROM	A	20	342	54	17	1	11	39	29	73	1	1	.293/.360/.463
2018	BRV	A+	20	90	3	7	0	0	10	6	16	0	0	.253/.300/.337
2019	BRV	A+	21	207	26	11	0	3	22	14	44	0	0	.263/.324/.368
2019	MIS	AA	21	209	24	9	0	3	17	15	40	0	0	.246/.306/.340
2020	ATL	MLB	22	251	24	13	1	6	27	15	64	0	0	.245/.296/.383

Comparables: Abiatal Avelino, Meibrys Viloria, Jacob Nottingham

YEAR	TEAM	P. COUNT	FRM RUNS	BLK RUNS	THRW RUNS	TOT RUNS
2019	MIS	6064	-0.2	0.0	0.0	0.6
2020	ATL	9182	-2.2	-0.3	0.1	-2.3

Contreras did about as well as one could expect from a raw, 21-year-old catcher getting assigned to Double-A. He showed glimpses of the talent that put him on the prospect map at lower levels last year while reminding everyone that most catchers simply take longer to develop. The younger brother of Willson continues to boast impressive physical abilities behind the plate for potential above-average to plus defensive tools, including a cannon arm. It'll take time to mold those natural abilities, especially as he works on quieting his receiving and shoring up his blocking, but it's the type of clay that any development staff would love to have. Same deal at the plate, where he's raw but has the eye and swing to develop into an average hitter with above-average pop. Treat him right with his assignments and the final product has exciting, everyday potential.

YEAR	TEAM	LVL	AGE	PA	DRC+	VORP	BABIP	BRR	FRAA	WARP
2017	DNV	RK	19	198	133	19.2	.326	-0.4	C(35): -0.5	1.4
2018	ROM	A	20	342	138	23.3	.351	-0.9	C(43): -0.3	2.2
2018	BRV	A+	20	90	103	2.5	.309	-0.3	C(20): -0.4	0.3
2019	BRV	A+	21	207	112	6.6	.329	-0.2	C(43): -0.8	1.0
2019	MIS	AA	21	209	99	8.4	.295	0.8	C(52): -1.1	0.9
2020	ATL	MLB	22	251	76	-0.2	.312	-0.4	C -3	-0.3

Michael Harris RF

Born: 03/07/01   Age: 19   Bats: L   Throws: L
Height: 6'0"   Weight: 195   Origin: Round 3, 2019 Draft (#98 overall)

YEAR	TEAM	LVL	AGE	PA	R	2B	3B	HR	RBI	BB	K	SB	CS	AVG/OBP/SLG
2019	BRA	RK	18	119	15	6	3	2	16	9	20	5	2	.349/.403/.514
2019	ROM	A	18	93	11	2	1	0	11	9	22	3	0	.183/.269/.232
2020	*ATL*	*MLB*	*19*	*251*	*22*	*11*	*1*	*3*	*22*	*23*	*72*	*3*	*1*	*.229/.304/.335*

Comparables: Justin Williams, J.P. Crawford, David Dahl

They say patience is a virtue because it sometimes produces solid major leaguers out of raw prep players. Pretty sure that's how the saying goes. It certainly applies to Harris, who is an above-average athlete with a cannon arm but will need time to develop the bat. He passed on the chance to be a two-way college player by signing with the Braves after being taken in the third round, and they liked what they saw on the position-player side. He's not a burner but has average speed and above-average range, which he'll need to use in center field to maximize his value. He could grow into above-average raw power. The question is how much Harris will hit, and it'll remain the question for some time as he needs to cut down the swing and find a more consistent bat path. Hit development would give Harris potential average or better tools across the board, and that's worth being patient.

YEAR	TEAM	LVL	AGE	PA	DRC+	VORP	BABIP	BRR	FRAA	WARP
2019	BRA	RK	18	119	138	11.3	.414	0.3	CF(19): 1.4, RF(3): -0.5	0.8
2019	ROM	A	18	93	58	-4.5	.246	-0.7	RF(18): 5.1, CF(4): 0.8	0.4
2020	*ATL*	*MLB*	*19*	*251*	*73*	*-0.8*	*.321*	*0.0*	*CF 1, RF 1*	*0.2*

Greyson Jenista OF
Born: 12/07/96   Age: 23   Bats: L   Throws: R
Height: 6'3"   Weight: 210   Origin: Round 2, 2018 Draft (#49 overall)

YEAR	TEAM	LVL	AGE	PA	R	2B	3B	HR	RBI	BB	K	SB	CS	AVG/OBP/SLG
2018	DNV	RK	21	47	10	1	0	3	7	6	9	0	1	.250/.348/.500
2018	ROM	A	21	130	20	5	3	1	23	10	17	4	1	.333/.377/.453
2018	BRV	A+	21	74	3	3	1	0	4	7	15	0	0	.152/.230/.227
2019	BRV	A+	22	231	24	14	1	4	29	27	70	1	4	.223/.312/.361
2019	MIS	AA	22	256	18	4	1	5	26	27	75	2	4	.243/.324/.338
2020	ATL	MLB	23	251	23	11	1	6	25	19	83	2	1	.219/.281/.351

Comparables: Bubba Starling, Michael Hermosillo, Joe Benson

Jenista is an enigma wrapped in a conundrum. His build and profile are made for a corner masher who doesn't clog the bases and offers value across all five tools. The problem is that he isn't tapping into the plus-or-better raw power because his swing isn't allowing it. He entered the pro ranks with a long, flat bat path and tons of moving parts, which he was able to get away with in his initial full-season taste just like he did in college. Swing tinkering and better competition has caught up to him as he's progressed, but he's far from being a lost cause and the Braves continue to show how much they like him by moving him up the ranks. Jenista still has the chance to be a low-end regular or platoon type. Those tweaks just need to start taking root.

YEAR	TEAM	LVL	AGE	PA	DRC+	VORP	BABIP	BRR	FRAA	WARP
2018	DNV	RK	21	47	128	2.2	.250	0.0	RF(7): 2.6, LF(2): 0.6	0.5
2018	ROM	A	21	130	143	7.5	.373	0.2	RF(30): -0.4	0.8
2018	BRV	A+	21	74	33	-5.8	.192	-0.6	RF(14): -0.8, CF(1): 0.0	-0.5
2019	BRV	A+	22	231	100	1.5	.315	-3.1	RF(40): -1.6, CF(8): -0.1	-0.1
2019	MIS	AA	22	256	98	5.8	.333	-2.9	LF(30): -4.4, RF(27): 0.4	-0.3
2020	ATL	MLB	23	251	68	-2.9	.314	-0.4	RF 1, LF -1	-0.3

Shea Langeliers C

Born: 11/18/97 Age: 22 Bats: R Throws: R
Height: 6'0" Weight: 190 Origin: Round 1, 2019 Draft (#9 overall)

YEAR	TEAM	LVL	AGE	PA	R	2B	3B	HR	RBI	BB	K	SB	CS	AVG/OBP/SLG
2019	ROM	A	21	239	27	13	0	2	34	17	55	0	0	.255/.310/.343
2020	ATL	MLB	22	251	21	12	1	4	23	15	76	2	1	.219/.270/.330

Comparables: Eddy Rodriguez, Tomás Nido, Elias Díaz

Let's get the obvious part out of the way first: Langeliers is a major-league defensive catcher with at least an above-average glove and a plus arm. He was probably the best defender behind the plate in the entire organization, majors included, the day he was drafted. The question is how much he'll hit. (How many times do we say that about prospects?) He has a surprisingly quick stroke and makes loud contact on the barrel. He's also over-aggressive at times. Developing an eye at the plate is the task going forward, as that would allow the above-average raw power to play in games. Improvements in that area would make Langeliers a standout everyday catcher in the big leagues, but he's a major-league quality backstop based on defense alone.

YEAR	TEAM	LVL	AGE	PA	DRC+	VORP	BABIP	BRR	FRAA	WARP
2019	ROM	A	21	239	100	4.9	.325	-1.3	C(41): 0.8	0.9
2020	ATL	MLB	22	251	60	-4.9	.303	0.0	C 0	-0.5

Cristian Pache CF

Born: 11/19/98 Age: 21 Bats: R Throws: R
Height: 6'2" Weight: 185 Origin: International Free Agent, 2015

YEAR	TEAM	LVL	AGE	PA	R	2B	3B	HR	RBI	BB	K	SB	CS	AVG/OBP/SLG
2017	ROM	A	18	514	60	13	8	0	42	39	104	32	14	.281/.335/.343
2018	BRV	A+	19	387	46	20	5	8	40	15	69	7	6	.285/.311/.431
2018	MIS	AA	19	109	10	3	1	1	7	5	28	0	2	.260/.294/.337
2019	MIS	AA	20	433	50	28	8	11	53	34	104	8	11	.278/.340/.474
2019	GWN	AAA	20	105	13	8	1	1	8	9	18	0	0	.274/.337/.411
2020	ATL	MLB	21	154	15	8	1	4	17	9	39	3	2	.251/.299/.401

Comparables: Ronald Acuña Jr., Jake Bauers, Freddie Freeman

Pache's tools outside the box are so good, he can fall short of his hitting potential and still be a star at the highest level. Think about that. The guy can fall short of expectations at perhaps the most important tool for position players and he can still produce star-level WARP. That's because his center field defense nearly breaks the scouting scale and he's not even done there. He pairs it with a double-plus arm for a huge weapon up the middle, and he uses double-plus speed to range better than almost anyone in the game at any level. As for the hitting part he might fail at, he's made big strides there by solidifying his lower half, adding lift and creating a more optimal bat path to meet the ball out front and tap into his above-average raw power. At this point, it's a fairly decent bet that his aggressiveness and swing-and-miss will limit his hit utility, but as long as he stays above water at the plate, he's going to make more highlight-reel plays than MLB producers know what to do with. It's about to happen, too.

YEAR	TEAM	LVL	AGE	PA	DRC+	VORP	BABIP	BRR	FRAA	WARP
2017	ROM	A	18	514	100	22.0	.360	5.8	CF(116): 27.8, RF(2): 0.0	5.2
2018	BRV	A+	19	387	114	14.7	.330	-1.1	CF(93): 3.9	2.1
2018	MIS	AA	19	109	69	-0.6	.347	-0.5	CF(28): 1.3	0.1
2019	MIS	AA	20	433	139	30.2	.351	-1.7	CF(57): 1.6, RF(23): 3.3	3.3
2019	GWN	AAA	20	105	90	1.2	.329	-0.9	CF(23): -3.2, RF(3): 3.3	0.2
2020	ATL	MLB	21	154	81	0.8	.320	-0.2	CF 1, RF 1	0.3

Braden Shewmake SS

Born: 11/19/97 Age: 22 Bats: L Throws: R
Height: 6'4" Weight: 190 Origin: Round 1, 2019 Draft (#21 overall)

YEAR	TEAM	LVL	AGE	PA	R	2B	3B	HR	RBI	BB	K	SB	CS	AVG/OBP/SLG
2019	ROM	A	21	226	37	18	2	3	39	21	29	11	3	.318/.389/.473
2019	MIS	AA	21	52	7	0	0	0	1	4	11	2	0	.217/.288/.217
2020	ATL	MLB	22	251	22	12	1	4	24	15	54	2	1	.233/.288/.350

Comparables: Darnell Sweeney, Donovan Solano, Gift Ngoepe

Atlanta's selection of Shewmake 21st overall in the 2019 draft came out of left field. Well, not literally—he's an infielder. The surprises weren't over when he went to Rome and showed potential average or better tools in all areas except power, boosting his post-draft stock and flying into the organization's top 10 prospects. The lanky Aggie is fluid at shortstop with enough arm for the left side, and he's equally fluid at the plate with a flat plane and contact approach. The ceiling is limited because there's no standout tool, but he squeezes the last drop out of every tool, including what could be an above-average bat. That will send him to the majors in at least a utility role in short order.

YEAR	TEAM	LVL	AGE	PA	DRC+	VORP	BABIP	BRR	FRAA	WARP
2019	ROM	A	21	226	162	25.7	.359	3.5	SS(38): 0.0	2.5
2019	MIS	AA	21	52	58	-0.9	.278	0.7	SS(14): 1.8	0.3
2020	ATL	MLB	22	251	70	-1.6	.286	0.0	SS 2	0.1

Drew Waters OF

Born: 12/30/98 Age: 21 Bats: B Throws: R
Height: 6'2" Weight: 183 Origin: Round 2, 2017 Draft (#41 overall)

YEAR	TEAM	LVL	AGE	PA	R	2B	3B	HR	RBI	BB	K	SB	CS	AVG/OBP/SLG
2017	BRA	RK	18	58	13	3	1	2	10	7	11	2	1	.347/.448/.571
2017	DNV	RK	18	166	20	11	1	2	14	16	59	4	2	.255/.331/.383
2018	ROM	A	19	365	58	32	6	9	36	21	72	20	5	.303/.353/.513
2018	BRV	A+	19	133	14	7	3	0	3	8	33	3	0	.268/.316/.374
2019	MIS	AA	20	454	63	35	9	5	41	28	121	13	6	.319/.366/.481
2019	GWN	AAA	20	119	17	5	0	2	11	11	43	3	0	.271/.336/.374
2020	ATL	MLB	21	251	25	16	2	6	28	15	84	4	1	.258/.310/.417

Comparables: Jorge Bonifacio, Travis Snider, Andrew Lambo

Those driving the Waters train have likely echoed the old saying, "hitters gonna hit," a few times already. It's understandable, because Waters is super aggressive at the plate and relies heavily on finding the barrel at an extremely high rate. And it's worked at every stop so far—including a brief taste of Triple-A before he could legally drink. Waters has the glove and range to play center field but hasn't done it in the Braves organization because of center fielder extraordinaire Cristian Pache, and while he's not a burner, he'll steal some bases to boot. He's a line-drive dude with the occasional eye-popping exit velocity, so the home run numbers won't match the raw power unless a tweak is made and he tones back the approach. Even so, put it all together and this is the profile of an above-average regular in the bigs. Braves scouting won't stop, can't stop.

YEAR	TEAM	LVL	AGE	PA	DRC+	VORP	BABIP	BRR	FRAA	WARP
2017	BRA	RK	18	58	126	7.9	.417	0.8	CF(9): -1.6, RF(3): 0.7	0.2
2017	DNV	RK	18	166	84	5.9	.409	-1.3	CF(35): -4.6	-0.3
2018	ROM	A	19	365	143	31.6	.362	3.9	CF(83): -0.6	3.2
2018	BRV	A+	19	133	92	4.6	.363	0.0	CF(30): -1.5, RF(1): -0.1	0.2
2019	MIS	AA	20	454	143	36.7	.436	-3.3	LF(54): 6.3, CF(38): 7.0	4.2
2019	GWN	AAA	20	119	79	-1.1	.429	0.7	RF(16): 2.1, LF(7): 0.4	0.3
2020	ATL	MLB	21	251	88	4.2	.380	0.1	CF 2, LF 2	0.8

Ian Anderson RHP

Born: 05/02/98   Age: 22   Bats: R   Throws: R
Height: 6'3"   Weight: 170   Origin: Round 1, 2016 Draft (#3 overall)

YEAR	TEAM	LVL	AGE	W	L	SV	G	GS	IP	H	HR	BB/9	K/9	K	GB%	BABIP
2017	ROM	A	19	4	5	0	20	20	83	69	0	4.7	11.0	101	50%	.345
2018	BRV	A+	20	2	6	0	20	20	100	73	2	3.6	10.6	118	47%	.282
2018	MIS	AA	20	2	1	0	4	4	19^1	14	0	4.2	11.2	24	48%	.304
2019	MIS	AA	21	7	5	0	21	21	111	82	8	3.8	11.9	147	46%	.287
2019	GWN	AAA	21	1	2	0	5	5	24^2	23	5	6.6	9.1	25	39%	.277
2020	ATL	MLB	22	3	4	0	22	11	57	55	7	3.6	9.9	62	42%	.316

Comparables: Alex Reyes, Archie Bradley, Jake Thompson

Atlanta's prep-pitching-heavy 2016 draft crop is collectively knocking on the door to consistent major-league production, which is a feat to behold considering the risk of popping prep arms early. Anderson was the headliner of that group and remains the face of it with three major-league offerings in his pocket. Does he have the high spin rates that the kids are buzzing about these days? Not really, but his stuff plays because of a tough arm angle and the ability to pair a plus changeup with a hard, sinking fastball. He doesn't have much room for error because his raw stuff isn't elite, but the successful Double-A jump showed he has enough command to live with what he's got, which is likely in the mid-rotation range.

YEAR	TEAM	LVL	AGE	WHIP	ERA	DRA	WARP	MPH	FB%	WHF	CSP
2017	ROM	A	19	1.35	3.14	3.80	1.4				
2018	BRV	A+	20	1.13	2.52	2.75	3.0				
2018	MIS	AA	20	1.19	2.33	3.29	0.5				
2019	MIS	AA	21	1.16	2.68	3.80	1.6				
2019	GWN	AAA	21	1.66	6.57	4.87	0.4				
2020	ATL	MLB	22	1.37	4.14	4.23	0.9				

Kyle Muller LHP

Born: 10/07/97 Age: 22 Bats: R Throws: L
Height: 6'6" Weight: 225 Origin: Round 2, 2016 Draft (#44 overall)

YEAR	TEAM	LVL	AGE	W	L	SV	G	GS	IP	H	HR	BB/9	K/9	K	GB%	BABIP
2017	DNV	RK	19	1	1	0	11	11	47²	43	5	3.4	9.3	49	40%	.284
2018	ROM	A	20	3	0	0	6	6	30	24	3	2.4	6.9	23	54%	.253
2018	BRV	A+	20	4	2	0	14	14	80²	80	2	3.6	8.8	79	42%	.350
2018	MIS	AA	20	4	1	0	5	5	29	22	3	1.9	8.4	27	40%	.244
2019	MIS	AA	21	7	6	0	22	22	111²	81	5	5.5	9.7	120	41%	.284
2020	ATL	MLB	22	1	1	0	3	3	16	16	2	3.8	8.4	15	39%	.302

Comparables: Eduardo Rodriguez, Jake Thompson, Génesis Cabrera

Muller was a dude when the Braves picked him in the second round a few years back, but he turned himself into a Dude after a velocity training program upped his fastball by several ticks to sit mid-90s and bump higher. He's always had that kind of velocity in him, as Muller is massive and physical on the mound. He found that extra oomph and saw his fastball bump to plus potential to pair with a changeup that can boast the same projection. Muller won't command his way to a front-end starter future though, and that's what has evaluators thinking of him as a dominant reliever. The way starters are handled these days, though, one could envision Muller shoving for four or five innings at the time. Either way, he's going to throw impactful major-league innings with live stuff from the left side.

YEAR	TEAM	LVL	AGE	WHIP	ERA	DRA	WARP	MPH	FB%	WHF	CSP
2017	DNV	RK	19	1.28	4.15	3.39	1.4				
2018	ROM	A	20	1.07	2.40	4.18	0.4				
2018	BRV	A+	20	1.39	3.24	4.91	0.4				
2018	MIS	AA	20	0.97	3.10	3.48	0.6				
2019	MIS	AA	21	1.33	3.14	4.85	0.1				
2020	ATL	MLB	22	1.43	4.61	4.69	0.2				

Darren O'Day   RHP

Born: 10/22/82 Age: 37 Bats: R Throws: R
Height: 6'4" Weight: 220 Origin: Undrafted Free Agent, 2006

YEAR	TEAM	LVL	AGE	W	L	SV	G	GS	IP	H	HR	BB/9	K/9	K	GB%	BABIP
2017	BAL	MLB	34	2	3	2	64	0	60^1	41	8	3.6	11.3	76	48%	.256
2018	BAL	MLB	35	0	2	2	20	0	20	18	3	1.8	12.1	27	26%	.326
2019	ATL	MLB	36	0	0	0	8	0	5^1	3	0	1.7	10.1	6	23%	.231
2020	ATL	MLB	37	1	1	0	27	0	28	26	6	2.7	9.4	30	38%	.268

Comparables: Mariano Rivera, Rafael Soriano, J.J. Putz

It would be understandable if casual Braves fans figured that O'Day was just a rumor or a myth—one of those players who was doomed to remember some guys status while actually still being active. However, injuries can't keep a good pitcher down forever and O'Day returned to the mound just in time to get a handful of innings in during September and the playoffs. Even though he only made a cameo, it was the type of cameo that makes you want to lock up said player swiftly at the start of the offseason. He'll no longer be talked about in hushed tones as if he's a spirit that is still lurking, although opposing left-handed batters may still question his existence as they're unlikely to see him much.

YEAR	TEAM	LVL	AGE	WHIP	ERA	DRA	WARP	MPH	FB%	WHF	CSP
2017	BAL	MLB	34	1.08	3.43	3.14	1.4	89.4	53.8	11.8	42.5
2018	BAL	MLB	35	1.10	3.60	3.67	0.3	88.8	52.3	13.2	51.7
2019	ATL	MLB	36	0.75	1.69	5.03	0.0	88.4	55.1	17.9	48.4
2020	ATL	MLB	37	1.20	4.17	4.44	0.3	87.8	52.2	12.4	46.9

Victor Vodnik RHP
Born: 10/09/99   Age: 20   Bats: R   Throws: R
Height: 6'0"   Weight: 200   Origin: Round 14, 2018 Draft (#412 overall)

YEAR	TEAM	LVL	AGE	W	L	SV	G	GS	IP	H	HR	BB/9	K/9	K	GB%	BABIP
2019	ROM	A	19	1	3	3	23	3	67^1	55	1	3.2	9.2	69	53%	.303
2020	ATL	MLB	20	2	2	0	33	0	35	34	5	3.9	7.8	30	48%	.289

Comparables: Eduardo Sanchez, Edgar Garcia, Dustin Antolin

Vodnik was more whisper and legend than real human after getting drafted in the 14th round in 2018. A poor spring dropped his draft stock and the Braves pounced on the lottery ticket, immediately reaping benefits when his stuff shot upward in instructs. That drew the whispers about what this guy, with the name that's fun to say, could do in full-season ball. Vodnik didn't disappoint in Rome, pumping mid-90s heat, consistently touching 97 and 98 and flashing a solid breaking ball. Atlanta limited his innings and he missed all of July because of injury, but he came back strong and should see slight increases in usage as he goes level by level. He comes from a high slot that limits his movement, but the fastball is live and he has the stuff to thrive in an impactful relief role.

YEAR	TEAM	LVL	AGE	WHIP	ERA	DRA	WARP	MPH	FB%	WHF	CSP
2019	ROM	A	19	1.17	2.94	4.44	0.4				
2020	ATL	MLB	20	1.41	4.43	4.70	0.3				

Patrick Weigel   RHP

Born: 07/08/94   Age: 25   Bats: R   Throws: R
Height: 6'6"   Weight: 240   Origin: Round 7, 2015 Draft (#210 overall)

YEAR	TEAM	LVL	AGE	W	L	SV	G	GS	IP	H	HR	BB/9	K/9	K	GB%	BABIP
2017	MIS	AA	22	3	0	0	7	7	37^1	32	2	2.7	9.2	38	37%	.300
2017	GWN	AAA	22	3	2	0	8	8	41	42	5	3.7	6.6	30	44%	.301
2019	MIS	AA	24	0	1	0	7	7	15^2	8	0	5.2	9.2	16	54%	.205
2019	GWN	AAA	24	6	1	0	21	11	63^1	42	9	4.5	7.8	55	40%	.208
2020	ATL	MLB	25	1	2	0	14	3	28	28	4	3.9	7.9	24	40%	.300

Comparables: Keyvius Sampson, Stephen Gonsalves, Ryan Helsley

Congratulations are in order for Weigel, who made it to the major leagues in 2019 after losing most of his 2018 season due to Tommy John surgery. It'll be hard to find video evidence of Weigel in the big leagues since he didn't make a single appearance (despite being called up twice), but he got to put the uniform on and realize a lifelong dream. After getting through 2019 with a clean bill of health while being guided through most of the season on a pitch limit, the next step for Weigel is to break those chains and show what he can really do with his high-octane fastball and biting slider. The next time he makes the big leagues, you won't have to look hard to find video of him being there—he'll be the center of attention.

YEAR	TEAM	LVL	AGE	WHIP	ERA	DRA	WARP	MPH	FB%	WHF	CSP
2017	MIS	AA	22	1.15	2.89	4.26	0.4				
2017	GWN	AAA	22	1.44	5.27	5.28	0.2				
2019	MIS	AA	24	1.09	1.72	3.21	0.3				
2019	GWN	AAA	24	1.17	2.98	3.03	2.2				
2020	ATL	MLB	25	1.47	5.12	5.09	0.2				

Atlanta Braves 2020

LINEOUTS

Hitters

HITTER	POS	TEAM	LVL	AGE	PA	R	2B	3B	HR	RBI	BB	K	SB	CS	AVG/OBP/SLG	DRC+	WARP
CJ Alexander	INF	MIS	AA	22	78	6	1	0	2	7	8	25	0	0	.103/.195/.206	39	-0.2
	INF	BRV	A+	22	74	4	1	0	0	1	14	18	3	1	.133/.297/.150	102	0.3
Mahki Backstrom	1B	BRA	Rk	17	82	8	5	0	2	8	12	27	1	0	.300/.402/.457	113	0.2
Bryce Ball	1B	DNV	Rk+	20	173	37	12	0	13	38	22	30	0	0	.324/.410/.676	173	1.5
	1B	ROM	A	20	90	14	6	0	4	14	4	20	0	0	.337/.367/.547	154	0.4
Justin Dean	CF	ROM	A	22	503	85	18	9	9	46	62	115	47	10	.284/.386/.431	141	4.3
Lucas Duda	1B	OMA	AAA	33	46	6	3	0	1	4	4	13	0	0	.286/.348/.429	75	-0.1
	1B	GWN	AAA	33	68	3	1	0	1	5	6	21	0	0	.140/.235/.211	43	-0.3
	1B	KCA	MLB	33	119	7	4	0	4	15	11	32	0	0	.171/.252/.324	78	-0.2
Trey Harris	OF	ROM	A	23	230	38	14	4	8	44	20	32	4	4	.366/.437/.594	207	2.7
	OF	MIS	AA	23	156	15	7	3	2	12	4	33	1	2	.281/.318/.411	91	-0.1
	OF	BRV	A+	23	139	20	5	0	4	17	12	26	3	0	.303/.388/.443	145	0.7
Alex Jackson	C	ATL	MLB	23	15	0	0	0	0	0	1	5	0	0	.000/.133/.000	77	0.1
	C	GWN	AAA	23	345	52	9	0	28	65	20	118	1	0	.229/.313/.533	106	3.1
John Ryan Murphy	C	GWN	AAA	28	50	5	0	0	1	3	2	13	0	0	.170/.220/.234	31	-0.1
	C	RNO	AAA	28	136	26	7	0	9	26	12	34	0	0	.250/.316/.524	92	0.5
	C	ARI	MLB	28	69	9	3	0	4	7	6	28	0	0	.177/.250/.419	68	0.2
	C	ATL	MLB	28	1	0	0	0	0	0	0	0	0	0	.000/.000/.000	143	0.0
Rafael Ortega	LF	GWN	AAA	28	493	83	34	3	21	58	59	95	14	7	.285/.373/.524	121	3.3
	LF	ATL	MLB	28	96	7	3	0	2	10	8	22	3	0	.205/.271/.307	75	-0.1
Beau Philip	SS	DNV	Rk+	20	239	27	6	0	4	20	26	51	5	5	.193/.297/.280	72	0.3
Jefrey Ramos	LF	BRV	A+	20	498	49	16	4	9	56	30	99	1	1	.241/.291/.352	94	-1.0

You'll be hard pressed to find a more unlucky, injury-plagued 2019 season than **CJ Alexander**'s, but maybe the baseball gods were angry for how easy he was making the sport look in the lower levels in 2018. ⓧ **Mahki Backstrom** is the poster child for Atlanta's 2019 draft strategy of late-round fliers on athletes with long developmental roads ahead of them. It's fun when one of these lands, especially when they're accompanied by an 80-grade name. ⓧ The biggest question surrounding **Bryce Ball**, who already boasted the biggest power in Atlanta's system after the 2019 draft, isn't his ultimate future but why he was picked so low. The kid is huge, hits tanks and is going to rocket up prospect lists, defense be damned. ⓧ **Justin Dean**'s feet on the basepaths are hotter than an overheated microwave sausage biscuit. Unlike the breakfast sandwich, Dean, a speedy fourth outfielder type, can potentially live up to expectations. ⓧ At a time in this country when most elected officials think leadership is a boat, we say good on **Lucas Duda** for extending his big-league career by another year on the strength of his vibes. ⓧ **Trey Harris** just won't stop hitting and maximizing his prospect value, which is fun to watch from a 32nd-round pick and senior sign with what's now a major-league future and fewer doubters by the day. ⚾ If you want a prime example of what the juiced baseball was like in Triple-A last season, **Alex Jackson** hit 28 homers in just 345 plate appearances. It'll be a miracle if he can ever replicate that at the major league level. ⚾ The man of many first names is a solid defensive catcher who can be trusted behind the plate. When it comes to what **John Ryan Murphy** can do for you at the plate with a bat in his hand, it's a completely different story and explains why he's in third-catcher purgatory. ⚾ If someone ever asks you who hit a game-winning grand slam on August 19, 2019 to defeat the Los Angeles Dodgers, you can now say that it was **Rafael Ortega**. Do with that information what you will. ⚾ **Beau Philip** became Atlanta's second-round beau in 2019 and offers some pop up the middle, but his hand path to the zone might necessitate a future tweak to get to that power more efficiently. ⚾ **Jefrey Ramos**, a bat-first corner prospect with diminishing value, ended up lost while trying to navigate through Florida, which has probably happened to a lot of us at some point.

Atlanta Braves 2020

Pitchers

PITCHER	TEAM	LVL	AGE	W	L	SV	G	GS	IP	H	HR	BB/9	K/9	K	GB%	WHIP	ERA	DRA	WARP
Jerry Blevins	LVG	AAA	35	0	0	0	7	0	10²	9	2	3.4	13.5	16	12%	1.22	1.69	3.23	0.3
	ATL	MLB	35	1	0	1	45	0	32¹	25	5	4.5	10.3	37	29%	1.27	3.90	4.98	0.1
Thomas Burrows	MIS	AA	24	1	3	1	16	0	21	16	2	2.6	10.3	24	47%	1.05	3.86	3.56	0.3
	GWN	AAA	24	1	1	6	27	0	36	31	3	4.5	9.8	39	41%	1.36	4.75	3.51	0.9
Tucker Davidson	MIS	AA	23	7	6	0	21	21	110²	88	5	3.7	9.9	122	51%	1.20	2.03	4.43	0.7
	GWN	AAA	23	1	1	0	4	4	19	20	0	4.3	5.7	12	51%	1.53	2.84	5.48	0.2
Grant Dayton	GWN	AAA	31	0	1	0	22	0	26²	20	6	1.4	13.8	41	40%	0.90	3.04	2.52	1.0
	ATL	MLB	31	0	1	0	14	0	12	12	4	3.0	10.5	14	39%	1.33	3.00	4.01	0.2
Jasseel De La Cruz	ROM	A	22	0	1	0	4	4	18	19	1	2.5	11.0	22	53%	1.33	2.50	4.67	0.1
	BRV	A+	22	3	1	0	4	4	28	12	0	2.2	8.4	26	52%	0.68	1.93	2.44	0.9
	MIS	AA	22	4	7	0	17	16	87	71	7	3.8	7.6	73	46%	1.24	3.83	4.67	0.3
Daysbel Hernandez	BRV	A+	22	5	2	7	35	0	52²	34	2	3.9	12.0	70	38%	1.08	1.71	2.88	1.1
Jake Higginbotham	ROM	A	23	4	4	4	33	0	58²	52	5	4.0	9.7	63	49%	1.33	3.07	4.94	-0.1
Philip Pfeifer	BRV	A+	26	4	6	0	16	14	92	81	7	2.2	10.8	110	42%	1.13	3.23	3.86	1.3
	MIS	AA	26	1	2	0	11	4	34	25	2	4.2	9.5	36	40%	1.21	2.38	4.09	0.3
	GWN	AAA	26	1	0	0	3	0	7¹	7	1	3.7	16.0	13	53%	1.36	2.45	1.44	0.3
Trey Riley	ROM	A	21	2	7	0	17	12	58²	71	4	7.1	6.3	41	47%	1.99	7.67	8.24	-2.2
Chad Sobotka	GWN	AAA	25	2	1	2	17	0	20²	23	3	1.7	13.9	32	48%	1.31	4.79	3.14	0.6
	ATL	MLB	25	0	0	0	32	0	29	28	6	5.9	11.8	38	45%	1.62	6.21	4.51	0.3
Freddy Tarnok	BRA	Rk	20	0	1	0	3	3	8	3	1	1.1	10.1	9	50%	0.50	3.38	1.00	0.4
	BRV	A+	20	3	7	0	19	19	98	105	6	3.3	7.5	82	38%	1.44	4.87	6.06	-1.2
Jeremy Walker	MIS	AA	24	1	6	6	21	1	58²	56	2	0.8	8.7	57	57%	1.04	2.45	3.81	0.6
	GWN	AAA	24	2	1	1	11	0	22²	20	1	2.4	9.9	25	50%	1.15	3.97	2.87	0.7
	ATL	MLB	24	0	0	0	6	0	9¹	9	0	3.9	5.8	6	57%	1.39	1.93	5.49	0.0
Huascar Ynoa	BRV	A+	21	0	1	0	3	3	11	10	0	4.9	13.1	16	59%	1.45	3.27	3.91	0.2
	MIS	AA	21	1	2	1	6	0	13²	17	2	3.3	9.9	15	67%	1.61	5.27	5.49	-0.1
	GWN	AAA	21	3	5	0	17	14	72²	80	14	4.2	9.8	79	43%	1.57	5.33	5.06	1.1
	ATL	MLB	21	0	0	0	2	0	3	6	1	3.0	9.0	3	42%	2.33	18.00	6.70	0.0

Being a LOOGY in 2020 means that **Jerry Blevins** spent much of the offseason workshopping some new skills like faking an arm injury, throwing a punch or disappearing into a puff of smoke. ⓘ **Thomas Burrows** is running out of time to find the strike zone and a major-league relief role—which will have to come in that order—but he's a lefty with a plus slider so opportunities will most assuredly come. ⓘ Texas high school Tascosa's **Tucker Davidson** has a titillating, tailing heater, a tilting breaker and a teasing changeup, all of which took a step forward to put him at the doorstep to a major-league role. ⓘ If anybody can tell you the dangers of playing catch, it's **Grant Dayton**. He came out of one with a fractured big toe. The unfortunate miss cost him a month of what turned out to be a very underwhelming season. ⓪ For **Jasseel De La Cruz**, it was simply a matter of staying healthy for his lively stuff and major-league (relief) ability to shine through in a breakout prospect season, which is the case for many but actually happened for him. ⓪ **Daysbel Hernández** is a quick-armed, physical Cuban with a lively two-pitch mix that wasn't even close to tested in A-ball, but a trip to the Arizona Fall League should mean his plus name appears on a more suitable roster going forward. ⓪ **Jake Higginbotham** flashes a two-pitch mix from the left side that shows major-league potential, which makes the fact that he was relegated to the depths of the minors at 23 years old even more taxing on the brain than saying his last name. ⓪ Despite limiting runs fairly successfully, disturbing walk rates have always lain beneath the surface of **Philip Pfeifer**'s line. That changed in 2019 as a significant uptick in control meant that he was no longer flirting dangerously with too many baserunners and the ERA improved further as a result. ⓪ Safe to say that **Trey Riley**'s full-season debut—full of inconsistent stuff and injured list stints—could go in the trash and no one would miss it, but the potential for upper-90s heat and a sharp slider in short bursts will keep prospect hounds on his trail. ⓪ The good news is that **Chad Sobotka** got the opportunity to throw twice as many innings in 2019 than he did in 2018. Unfortunately, every single one of his stats went in the wrong direction. ⓪ **Freddy Tarnok**'s development journey toward a big-league staff is going to be long and arduous, but what's the fun in getting there easily? ⓪ **Jeremy Walker** spent 2019 making some serious improvement at both the Double-A and Triple-A levels. He was rewarded with a handful of big league appearances in 2019 and he'll be aiming for a steady bullpen role soon. ⓪ **Huascar Ynoa** was called up in 2019 for the first three major league innings of his career. That was enough time for him to give up a grand slam to Christian Yelich. Good morning, good afternoon and good night until we see you again, Huascar.

Braves Prospects

The State of the System
There are a lot of familiar names here, but they're still good prospects, and they are now close to helping a good major-league team.

The Top Ten

───── ★ ★ ★ *2020 Top 101 Prospect* **#22** ★ ★ ★ ─────

1 Cristian Pache OF   OFP: 70   ETA: 2020
Born: 11/19/98   Age: 21   Bats: R   Throws: R   Height: 6'2"   Weight: 185
Origin: International Free Agent, 2015

The Report: Signed as a raw, yet toolsy outfielder with an elite predilection defensively, Pache has improved each year offensively to round out his game as the top prospect in the organization and one of the best in baseball. It helps having an abundance of athleticism to draw from, as he's been able to maintain his dynamic body while adding strength. In the span of one season he put on 10-15 pounds of muscle on what was once a very thin frame, with still some room left to completely fill out.

It's always been a free-swinging approach that produces a lot of contact, but now the power is becoming more pronounced with the added strength. He's a fastball hunter with relatively quiet movements, employing a modest leg kick in fastball counts and shortening up against offspeed. Previously, he had a tendency to swing out of his shoes to generate more power, but as the body developed, he's been able to stay balanced through contact better without sacrificing power and also allowing to see the ball better.

The strikeouts will always be a concern given his approach, but the latest signs of improved plate discipline would be the finishing touches on the makings of a true five-tool player. With plus speed, a double-plus glove and throwing arm, Pache should be roaming the outfield very early in 2020. He saw time in all three outfield spots last season because of the current deployment of outfielders in Atlanta, but center field would be a natural fit. Alongside Ronald Acuña (and another prospect not much further down this list), Pache is poised to be part of an exciting trio of outfielders for years to come.

Variance: High. He has unteachable talent, but what remains to be taught is a honed approach that will inevitably determine just how high the ceiling is.

Mark Barry's Fantasy Take: *Finally* a super-toolsy and exciting outfielder in Atlanta. It's about time. Pache's defense is the marquee quality for sure, but for our purposes, his ceiling will depend on two things—1) whether he can curtail the Ks enough to unlock his power whilst (damn right, whilst) not sapping batting average, and 2) whether his elite speed can translate to stolen bases. That second part might be the most important, as Pache can definitely run, but snagged just eight bags in 19 tries this season. Upside is perhaps peak Ender Inciarte with 20+ homer pop. Downside is 2019 Ender Inciarte without steals.

★ ★ ★ *2020 Top 101 Prospect* **#38** ★ ★ ★

2. Ian Anderson   RHP   OFP: 60   ETA: 2020
Born: 05/02/98   Age: 22   Bats: R   Throws: R   Height: 6'3"   Weight: 170
Origin: Round 1, 2016 Draft (#3 overall)

The Report: The crown jewel of a deep pitching pipeline that Braves' player development keeps producing is tall righty Ian Anderson. He's one of a slough of pitching prospects drafted and developed in relatively short order, part of a talent class that ascended together to all reach Triple-A around their age-21 season. While his five-start stint in Gwinnett wasn't glamorous due to giving up the longball at an uncharacteristic clip, he's quietly amassed an impressive minor league resume chalking up strikeouts and preventing runs.

He stands much taller on the hill than his listed 6-foot-3, and with long levers and a high three-quarters arm slot he is able to get excellent plane on his fastball that sits 92-94 but can top out at 96 mph. The arm slot is key to Anderson's success, as it makes it difficult to square up the heater and also provides the unconventional shape he gets from his secondary offerings. The curveball is his best present offspeed pitch, and it has good tumbling finish in the zone, but the changeup flashes equal promise despite its inconsistencies with late sink.

What is left to accomplish prior to cracking the big league roster? He tends to nibble around the strike zone, which can lead to deep counts and inflated walk totals. The stuff is good enough to attack hitters and have more efficient outings, rather than relying on trying to strike out everybody. His late season struggle was one of the first of his professional career, so how he handles adversity will be something to monitor.

Variance: Medium. The mechanics are clean, even with a high delivery, and there's no history of arm issues. Like any young pitcher, especially one who is enduring a heavy innings workload for the first time in his life, there is always mild risk involved.

Mark Barry's Fantasy Take: When Anderson was drafted, I remember thinking "Huh, that seems like a reach. I don't know about that one, Braves." Well, I'm big enough to tell you that Past Mark is a dumb idiot. The extra walks are troubling, yes, but I can't think of five dynasty hurlers I'd rather have than Anderson.

─────── ★ ★ ★ *2020 Top 101 Prospect* **#42** ★ ★ ★ ───────

3 **Drew Waters   OF**   OFP: 60   ETA: 2020
Born: 12/30/98   Age: 21   Bats: B   Throws: R   Height: 6'2"   Weight: 183
Origin: Round 2, 2017 Draft (#41 overall)

The Report: Selected as one of the youngest players in the 2017 draft, Waters has done nothing but hit since joining the Braves, reaching Triple-A last year at 20 years old. The accelerated path is a product of his offensive potential as a switch-hitting doubles machine who is still tapping into his power. The question that confounds evaluators is whether the game power will ever be fully realized given his flat bat path and propensity to be out on his front leg, which saps potential power out of the swing. Regardless, he led the Southern League in hitting as one of its youngest players before his late season promotion to Gwinnett.

His hyper-aggressive approach leads to either hard contact early in the at-bat, or gets him quickly behind in the count where he's forced to battle. There's more fluidity from the left side where he's able to drop his hands quickly to meet the ball, whereas from the right-handed batter's box he looks more stiff and out of sync. It's fair to question how long he will continue switch-hitting given the disparity in platoon splits that are evident in each of his pro seasons.

Defensively, he is passable in every outfield spot, but given a future triumvirate of Cristian Pache and Ronald Acuña in Atlanta, he would likely be relegated to left field as the weakest glove of the three. He is far from a polished product, but the natural talent to hit line drives with regularity will have him knocking on the door of the majors in short order.

Variance: Very high. Depending on who you ask, Waters will either be a star at his peak or an average, everyday player. It all boils down to if the power arrives and the doubles turn into homers.

Mark Barry's Fantasy Take: I guess I shouldn't penalize Waters for not knowing who he is at 20 years old. In a dynasty setting, it would be nice to figure it out though. If he can scale back on the strikeouts while maintaining his efficiency on the bases, he's got OF2 upside. If he doesn't, well, he doesn't. He's still a top-20 dynasty prospect, so we're grading on a big curve here, but there is some downside if things don't click.

─────── ★ ★ ★ *2020 Top 101 Prospect* **#60** ★ ★ ★ ───────

4 **Kyle Muller   LHP**   OFP: 60   ETA: 2020
Born: 10/07/97   Age: 22   Bats: R   Throws: L   Height: 6'6"   Weight: 225
Origin: Round 2, 2016 Draft (#44 overall)

The Report: Big man, big fastball, big strikeouts, but also big walks. "Big" is the appropriate word when describing Kyle Muller—including his potential—but within a good 2019 campaign a troubling trend lurked. A slight up-tick in fastball velocity led to elevated strikeout totals but also an alarmingly high amount of walks issued compared to his previous body of work.

Regularly working in the mid-to-upper 90s, the southpaw unquestionably has a live arm, but the extra effort exerted to reach the high 90s more consistently has had a negative effect on his command. The overall package is that of a potential starter, with a breaking ball he can manipulate to have a slurvy break or tighter slider shape, and a changeup that took a big step forward to perhaps become his best secondary offering.

The frame is prototypical workhorse material, the stuff is obvious, but unless the walk totals go back to their pre-2019 average ratings, the question of a potential reliever profile begins to creep into the discussion.

Variance: Very high. The upside in Muller's game could push his grade even higher, but with the sudden increase in velocity and subsequent drop in command there is risk regarding his future role and inherent injury risk, too.

Mark Barry's Fantasy Take: If I had to guess, Muller's favorite Lou Reed song is "Walk on the Wild Side." I bet he also really enjoyed the White Walkers in *Game of Thrones*. He walks a lot of people, is what I'm saying. The talent is absolutely there for a top-100 dynasty prospect, but the extra free passes lead me to believe he could be a liability in the rate stats, expanding his floor to fantasy SP6ish or *gasp* a reliever.

───────── ★ ★ ★ *2020 Top 101 Prospect* **#77** ★ ★ ★ ─────────

5 **Shea Langeliers** C   OFP: 55   ETA: 2021
Born: 11/18/97   Age: 22   Bats: R   Throws: R   Height: 6'0"   Weight: 190
Origin: Round 1, 2019 Draft (#9 overall)

The Report: Atlanta was high on Langeliers and went all-in on the top defensive catcher in the 2019 draft class. He would've been the first backstop taken if not for a certain No. 1 overall pick. No catcher is ever a certainty coming through the minor leagues, but even a small hint of a productive bat will push Langeliers to the upper levels because of an impressive set of defensive tools. He has the makings of a plus glove with a strong feel to receive, solid footwork and an advanced ability to handle a game and pitching staff. He's a leader on the field. It also helps that he flashes plus-plus pop times and has an easy plus arm as one of the biggest weapons on the field. He has a strong catcher's frame with a durable lower half, but he's also more athletic than the typical backstop. At the plate, Langeliers has a surprisingly quick bat and sound swing geared for contact and gap power. His above-average raw power produces loud contact, but his first taste of pro ball left him between pitches at times and he pressed himself into over-aggressiveness. A quick, short stroke and aptitude are on his side and should be enough to reach average hit and power. That's enough to make Langeliers a glove-first starter.

Variance: Medium. Catchers can take a million different directions developmentally, but Langeliers can put you a little more at ease because of advanced, standout defense that will carry his profile.

Mark Barry's Fantasy Take: Glove-first, dynasty-catching prospects rank somewhere between Hall of Fame arguments and the Cleveland baseball team's spending habits on my list of least favorite things. Sure, he could eventually be a top-five backstop on the NL, but according to valuations czar Mike Gianella that's only good for the 91st most valuable hitter on the Senior Circuit. I like Langeliers more than the next catcher we'll get to on this list, but it's a low bar.

───── ★ ★ ★ *2020 Top 101 Prospect* **#89** ★ ★ ★ ─────

6
Kyle Wright   RHP   OFP: 60   ETA: 2018
Born: 10/02/95   Age: 24   Bats: R   Throws: R   Height: 6'4"   Weight: 200
Origin: Round 1, 2017 Draft (#5 overall)

The Report: David noted in this space last year that Wright is, on paper, "the ideal pitching prospect." He's certainly got an ideal build. He has the full four-pitch mix, and he's added a sinker. His mechanics are visually impressive and repeatable. He pitched well for three years in the SEC and went in the top five in his draft year. He moved through the minors quickly, making his major-league debut just fifteen months after he was drafted. Why, then, has he been slipping just a little each year for us?

The whole is adding up to be a bit less than the sum of the parts, I suppose, and it might be sending Wright on a different path than we expected. The fastball is still in the same 92-96 velocity band where it's always been, touching a tick or two higher. Yet his fastball command has never advanced far enough for it to play up, and it gets hit just a little more than you'd like. His slider velocity has ticked up into the 88-90 range, and it's gotten more cuttery, to the point that Wright has referred to it as both a slider and a cutter. It's his best offspeed, a true out pitch…and also the only one that projects as an above-average pitch right now. Neither his curve nor his change has advanced to be a reliable third offering.

So what we have, as he's on the precipice of fully graduating to the majors, is a pitcher reliant on his mid-90s fastball and power slider, with command and third pitch questions, who looked generally dominant in September short relief. Let's pretend he's not Kyle Wright, former Vanderbilt ace and fifth-overall pick and mound adonis, and just Kyle Wright, pitching prospect. Doesn't that sound a whole lot like a future closer instead of a mid-rotation starter to you?

Variance: Medium. Wright has already reached an up-and-down role, and he's likely to be at least a decent major-league pitcher as soon as 2020. There's some volatility in terms of role, and to some extent there's the whole "mid-rotation prospects rarely end up exactly turning into mid-rotation pitchers" thing going on here.

Mark Barry's Fantasy Take: One person that's probably psyched by the Braves signing ALL OF THE RELIEVERS this offseason has to be Wright. After getting rocked in his first big-league taste as a starter, he was relegated to a bullpen role down the stretch, and really has the stuff to be a late-inning star. He'll likely get the chance to start again now, and if he can hone a third pitch (which is, like, super easy, right?), fantasy SP4 is still the upside.

7 Bryse Wilson   RHP   OFP: 55   ETA: 2018
Born: 12/20/97   Age: 22   Bats: R   Throws: R   Height: 6'1"   Weight: 225
Origin: Round 4, 2016 Draft (#109 overall)

The Report: Wilson shot up from A-ball to the majors in 2018. 2019 was more of a consolidation year; he pitched well in Triple-A, but struggled in a handful of stints in the majors. In many ways, he's been in a similar pattern to Wright over the last year: he's slipped a little more in that he's failed to take a step forward. That said, unlike Wright, before 2019 he did actually make big strides from where he was on draft day.

He remains an extremely fastball-reliant pitcher at present, throwing it around 70 percent of the time in the majors so far. It's a very good fastball, thrown in the mid 90s with late life. But it's hard to thrive as a starting pitcher with that level of fastball usage. The slider and changeup both flash above-average, but neither is consistently there, and he doesn't reliably lean on either as a primary offspeed quite yet. Like Wright, it is possible that his future home is more in a late-inning relief role, especially given organizational pitching depth.

Wilson doesn't turn 22 until next month. There isn't a lot left for him to show in Triple-A. The Braves, who have four rotation spots locked up already by Mike Soroka, Mike Foltynewicz, Max Fried, and Cole Hamels, have multiple other Opening Day rotation candidates, including Wright, Touki Toussaint, and Sean Newcomb. So Wilson might get squeezed into the bullpen or even back to Triple-A; the 2020 Braves present a case where the needs of player development and a contending major-league roster might be at cross purposes.

Variance: Medium. Wilson has also reached an up-or-down role, and also is about ready. We do think he's a bit less likely to put it all together and end up higher than a mid-rotation type than Wright, which explains why he's behind him here.

Mark Barry's Fantasy Take: Wilson might be a prisoner of his organization, as he's probably ready to pitch full time in the big leagues, but the Braves are overflowing with options for back of the rotation starters. I think that's his role, though, as a sixth starter and a fantasy streamer. There's always going to be a guy like this on the wire.

8 William Contreras   C   OFP: 55   ETA: 2021
Born: 12/24/97   Age: 22   Bats: R   Throws: R   Height: 6'0"   Weight: 180
Origin: International Free Agent, 2015

The Report: The start of Contreras's season in High-A and the latter part in Double-A was a study in contrasts largely driven by confidence. In High-A, Contreras had a swagger that carried into every part of his game. He was an energetic and athletic player who led with his attitude and his play. His Double-A performance was an example of how important confidence is in a player's performance as he was noticeably more subdued in every area and his results suffered.

When at his best, Contreras has the makings of a solid defensive catcher. His arm is his best tool and he uses it liberally to keep runners honest. He has some work to do to refine his framing and blocking, but he has soft hands and quick feet and shows a willingness to work to improve. He projects as an above-average defender.

Offensively, Contreras has an athletic approach with a solid foundation. He has quick hands and slightly above-average bat speed. He struggles with timing and he likely needs an adjustment to get to more loft in his swing to access his power more efficiently.

Again, the difference in levels was interesting. At High-A, he was aggressive and that made him susceptible to offspeed pitches, especially in higher-leverage at-bats. At Double-A, he was less aggressive, took more pitches and had less swing-and-miss, but the quality of his contact was not as consistent.

Contreras is just a few adjustments away from becoming a catcher who can make an impact on both sides of the ball. If he can also rediscover that swagger from early in the 2019 season, he will be on his way to becoming an above-average backstop.

Variance: High. Catching has a lot of moving parts.

Mark Barry's Fantasy Take: Is this the Golden Age for dynasty catching prospects? Almost certainly not, but also maybe. That's damning with faint praise, sure, as Contreras is probably a top-10 dynasty prospect behind the dish but probably doesn't have that same top-10 big-league upside.

9 Braden Shewmake SS
OFP: 50   ETA: 2021
Born: 11/19/97   Age: 22   Bats: L   Throws: R   Height: 6'4"   Weight: 190
Origin: Round 1, 2019 Draft (#21 overall)

The Report: The Braves surprised many by drafting Shewmake with their second first-round pick in 2019, but his early play appeared to vindicate the selection, as he garnered louder post-draft reports. The pre-draft grades seemed especially light on his defense, where he showed excellent feel at shortstop in his first pro assignment. The lanky Aggie has soft hands and ranges well for his length, helped in part by good instincts, and there's enough arm for any infield position. He'll always be lean and long, but he does enough on the first step and has the hands to play anywhere on the infield, more so on a regular basis at second or third and in a pinch at short. It's the same on the basepaths, where he's surprisingly quick down the line for solid-average run. Shewmake's top tool is a potential above-average hit based on excellent feel for the barrel. It's a simple, contact-oriented swing and approach that limits his game power to fringe-average, but he'll make consistent, hard contact and shoot the gaps often while running into the occasional blast. This is a pretty straightforward profile with fringe- to above-average tools across the board and the instincts to make them play at the highest level. It's not sexy but it's worthy of super-utility potential, and it shouldn't take long to happen.

Variance: Medium. He hasn't passed the upper-level test yet, but the advanced bat will play pretty quickly and get him to the majors.

Mark Barry's Fantasy Take: Shewmake seems to be missing a few letters from his name, but he didn't miss the chance to fly through the organization, reaching Double-A by the end of his draft year. If he continues the trajectory to super-utility stardom, he's an interesting name for deeper or onlies, but he's not shallow-mixed league relevant right now.

10 Jasseel De La Cruz   RHP   OFP: 50   ETA: 2020
Born: 06/26/97   Age: 23   Bats: R   Throws: R   Height: 6'1"   Weight: 215
Origin: International Free Agent, 2015

The Report: De La Cruz struggled with injuries in 2018 and was described on last year's Braves list by David Lee as "a raw power arm who could go in a million directions." Well, he was healthy in 2019, tossed 133 pretty good innings across three levels, and signs are pointing up. The underlying stuff profile is mostly the same, we just saw it across a longer body of work. De La Cruz pumps mid-90s heat with good extension and some deception, although there is a lot of effort to hit the upper end of that velocity range. The fastball command and control can be erratic, and the pitch can run a bit true. Despite his height, the extension and higher slot gives the pitch some plane, at least.

De La Cruz pairs the heater with a power slider that flashes plus and has gotten more consistent in 2019. It's easy to see it as a swing-and-miss pitch in the majors. His changeup is firm, regularly hitting 90 or higher, and he struggles to get it down in the zone, although on the rare occasions he does the pitch will show average dive. De La Cruz is still a raw power arm in some ways, but he's started to see on-field results. The reliever risk here is high, but he'd be a good reliever, and he's still young enough to project some command and changeup gains if so inclined.

Variance: Medium. De La Cruz's fastball/slider combo gives him a decent shot at some sort of major-league pen work, even with the quibbles about the command. He's already had Double-A success as well. Still, the overall profile is pretty raw and there's significant reliever risk given the delivery, command, and present changeup. That risk might manifest in making him merely an up-and-down frustrating pen arm that flashes for a month here and there.

Mark Barry's Fantasy Take: The range of outcomes for De La Cruz is breathtaking. If things shake right, he's a sneaky-good, mid-rotation option. If things break (hopefully not literally) wrong, he pitches a handful of middling innings out of the pen when called upon as an injury fill-in. I'd take a flier on him in leagues with 250 prospects or more, betting on continued development now that he's stringing together better health.

The Next Ten

11. Freddy Tarnok   RHP
Born: 11/24/98   Age: 21   Bats: R   Throws: R   Height: 6'3"   Weight: 185
Origin: Round 3, 2017 Draft (#80 overall)

Last year's report on Tarnok called him more of a "slow burn" than the pitching prospects ranked above him. That still fits him well after almost 100 innings of mixed results at High-A Florida this past season. He just turned 21 in November 2019, but it seems like he's been around longer because the Braves have worked him slowly after he didn't even turn to pitching until late in his prep days. He's still raw, but he's still throwing with an ideal pitcher's frame, and he still has stuff. The fastball has plus potential with mid-90s velocity in short bursts, while the curveball flashes above-average and can settle a tick below with further refinement. He's worked to get his changeup on par and it's always had that potential, but it's still a work in progress along with the ability to repeat his delivery. None of this sounds particularly thrilling, but one can see why the Braves are taking the time with Tarnok. He has standout arm strength and a great frame with fewer innings on the arm. The ceiling is still very high, like, impact starter high, but the gap is still very large and could ultimately push him to the bullpen.

12. Bryce Ball   1B
Born: 07/08/98   Age: 21   Bats: L   Throws: R   Height: 6'6"   Weight: 235
Origin: Round 24, 2019 Draft (#727 overall)

It's understandable if the first question that crosses your mind after watching Ball is how he ended up lasting until the 24th round. This is a massive kid who already has the biggest raw power in the system, perhaps alongside Alex Jackson. It's quite the find when an organization drafts a player that late and he immediately has a system's best tool, pushing 70. That high grade comes from size and natural strength, but it's not a muscled swing. His bat speed approaches above-average with good lift and separation. The bat speed can play down at times when he settles for contact to all fields, but it's a positive that he's capable of covering the plate well for his size and profile. It's not a boom-or-bust power profile because he's shown a feel to hit. Ball's defense is a different matter. He shows a lack of feel for first base with a hard glove and inconsistent footwork. It'll take time to develop his glove enough to be serviceable, and first base is his only option because of bottom-of-the-scale speed. Regardless of his defense, Ball has more than enough potential in his bat and power to force an organization to find a lineup spot for him. First base profiles are a tricky business for prospects, but the Braves found themselves a super-intriguing slugger who should rocket up this list in short order. It's not crazy to say he can become the best first base prospect in the game at some point.

13 Huascar Ynoa   RHP
Born: 05/28/98   Age: 22   Bats: R   Throws: R   Height: 6'3"   Weight: 175
Origin: International Free Agent, 2014

On June 16th, Ynoa made his major-league debut in Atlanta, mopping up the last two innings of a 15-1 blowout win over the Phillies. He spiked his first fastball at 98—nerves no doubt—and then proceeded to work his way through the Phillies lineup, pumping upper-90s heat, touching 99, and breaking off what Brooks thinks are a bunch of 86 and 87 mph curves, one of which ended up a nice souvenir—his first professional strikeout against Rhys Hoskins.

On July 17th, he found himself back in the majors, and promptly got shelled to the tune of six runs in one inning of work. Christian Yelich hit a laser beam grand slam off one of those power breakers that only bent. Major League Baseball is hard, my man.

Aside from those two games, Ynoa found himself starting at three levels of Braves affiliates, struggling to throw strikes, but missing plenty of bats when he was in the zone. It's power stuff—similar to De La Cruz—but even less refined and with greater command issues. Ynoa looks more like a reliever long term, but that fastball/breaking ball combo is deadly when he's right, and he only turned 21 a couple weeks before his major-league debut. That debut was perhaps a bit premature—Ynoa was added to the 40-man last season and the Braves needed an arm, but that June afternoon could be a preview of coming attractions and the trailer won't be misleading.

14 Alex Jackson   C
Born: 12/25/95   Age: 24   Bats: R   Throws: R   Height: 6'2"   Weight: 215
Origin: Round 1, 2014 Draft (#6 overall)

This has been quite a journey. You may remember Jackson as the sixth-overall pick in the 2014 Draft by the Mariners. He was a prep catcher then, but was immediately converted to the outfield under the idea that his bat was ahead of his glove. He ranked 94th on the 2015 101, and then proceeded to go out and hit .157 in his full-season debut in 2015, getting demoted back to extended spring training in late May. Suddenly the bat wasn't so advanced anymore, and after another season of slightly better muddling in 2016, the Mariners offloaded him to the Braves for well under sticker price. Atlanta immediately converted him back to catcher, and he's slowly filtered up through their system for the past three years, getting a couple cups of coffee in 2019. On some levels, the story has remained the same since his later days in the Seattle farm; he's still a good athlete with a big, strong frame and plus raw power, but major questions about his ability to make contact and hit for any average. It's a long swing and not always on balance. Yet two markers from his 2019 statistical performance paint a more optimistic picture: he hit 28 homers in just 345 Triple-A plate appearances, which is still a lot even given the Super Happy Fun Ball. Perhaps even more interestingly, he graded out as the best defensive catcher in Triple-A by FRAA. That's a level where we have pretty sticky framing stats. He also gunned out 50 percent of baserunners. That's enough pop and defense to give him some substantial upside, perhaps even still a good regular if he can keep the average high enough.

15 Victor Vodnik   RHP
Born: 10/09/99   Age: 20   Bats: R   Throws: R   Height: 6'0"   Weight: 200
Origin: Round 14, 2018 Draft (#412 overall)

Vodnik is an easy pick for future mover in the system because of a combination of impending graduations and his own rise in the minors. He doesn't get much love because he's a 6-foot right-hander with a bullpen future, but he has major-league stuff, enough command to make it work, and the mound presence to match. He was kept on a throwing schedule in his first full season and missed July but still threw 67 innings because of his multi-inning role, which serves him well as the type of arm that can toss a couple innings at the time. His fastball is 93-96 and touches 97 with riding life and effectiveness up and down the zone. He mixes two breaking balls between a short, hard slider and a power curve with downward break and solid-average depth, the latter flashing above-average. He'll also toss the occasional show-me changeup. Vodnik lacks height advantage but attacks hitters in all four quadrants with lively stuff and a quick arm. The easy call is middle relief, but he has the chance for late-innings impact.

16 Michael Harris   OF
Born: 03/07/01   Age: 19   Bats: L   Throws: L   Height: 6'0"   Weight: 195
Origin: Round 3, 2019 Draft (#98 overall)

After taking the high-floor college route with their first three picks in the 2019 draft, the Braves went back to their Georgia prep athlete roots by popping Harris in the third round and convincing him to pass on a Texas Tech commitment that probably would've led to two-way stardom. The Braves liked him at the plate and put him in right field full-time, where he was aggressively pushed to Low-A Rome for the final few weeks and he struggled to stay afloat. Harris is a raw product with the bat, at times getting caught between pitches and showing wrap and inconsistent bat paths. There's a lot to like, though, especially a feel for the barrel and loose hands that should help as he works to iron out his swing. His contact is loud and he'll grow into above-average raw power despite an average frame, a testament to his quick bat and strong wrists. Harris is a good athlete but not a burner, featuring average run times and solid- to above-average range in the outfield. A move to center field would boost his stock tremendously, but if he stays in right the bat and power will need to max out. His standout tool is at least a plus arm that profiles as a weapon in center or right. It's going to be a level-by-level process that'll take time and patience, but there's a lot to like with Harris, namely athleticism, a feel for the game, and a cannon for an arm.

17 Tucker Davidson   LHP
Born: 03/25/96   Age: 24   Bats: L   Throws: L   Height: 6'2"   Weight: 215
Origin: Round 19, 2016 Draft (#559 overall)

Perhaps no pitcher in the system, besides maybe De La Cruz, increased his stock this past season more than Davidson. Credit to the left-hander for recognizing that the full-time starter experiment was in danger of going off the rails. He put in the work to improve his arm strength and durability, and his stuff held deeper in starts this past season, resulting in a great year between the two highest levels of the minors and a 40-man roster spot. He saw an uptick in fastball velocity to pump mid-90s more often and he mixed his stuff more effectively between an average curve that flashes above and an improved changeup. There was little reason in 2018 to believe that Davidson had a chance to be a starter, but he's worked his way into that conversation. The fallback plan is still a lefty reliever with a hard fastball and solid curve, which could happen as soon as 2020, but he's now given the Braves a reason to see if he sticks as a starter at the highest level.

18 Patrick Weigel   RHP
Born: 07/08/94   Age: 25   Bats: R   Throws: R   Height: 6'6"   Weight: 240
Origin: Round 7, 2015 Draft (#210 overall)

If you're looking for someone to root for in this system, I recommend Weigel. He was an immediate seventh-round steal with explosive stuff who was knocking on the major-league door until he succumbed to Tommy John surgery and fell by the wayside. He reappeared late in 2018 with his velocity mostly back, but he was understandably rusty and expectations were all over the map entering 2019. He responded to Atlanta's faith (and a 40-man roster addition) by returning to the precipice of the majors with his mid-to-upper-90s fastball in short bursts and a sharp slider. It was never a given that Weigel would be a starter in the majors, and it now seems more likely that his ultimate role is in relief where he can let his velocity fly and cut his arsenal down. Weigel's stuff is late-innings worthy and he has nothing left to prove in Triple-A.

19 Greyson Jenista   OF
Born: 12/07/96   Age: 23   Bats: L   Throws: R   Height: 6'3"   Weight: 210
Origin: Round 2, 2018 Draft (#49 overall)

Jenista is a big, strong lefty-swinging power hitter. Though he is a bit more athletic than many other players with that physical profile, the power is his only standout tool and his development as a prospect is going to be all about how well he is able to get to that power in games. The other tools are mostly average. Defensively, he can play center in a pinch and he has just enough arm to play in right, but he's mostly a left fielder who should be able to make most of the plays there. He could see some time at first base at some point down the road as well.

At the plate, he starts with his hands very high and that leaves him a lot to accomplish to get his bat to the ball at the proper launch angle to find that plus raw power. To this point in his career, he has struggled to find the correct timing to do that with any consistency. When it does work, it's a thing of beauty. It is going to take a major adjustment, though, for him to get quicker to the ball, create a more power-efficient bat path and better manage what are becoming alarmingly high strikeout rates. Without that adjustment, Jenista's ceiling drops to just that of a platoon bat.

20 Trey Riley   RHP
Born: 04/21/98   Age: 22   Bats: L   Throws: R   Height: 6'3"   Weight: 205
Origin: Round 5, 2018 Draft (#142 overall)

The fifth-round pick in 2018 had a tough go-round in his first year of full-season ball. Riley struggled mightily with command throughout his abbreviated injury-riddled season, issuing 46 walks against 41 punchouts over 58 2/3 innings. His fastball sits 92-95 mph and comes in fairly straight. However, violent mechanics can lead to major command issues. Riley has fast arm action with a max-effort delivery, and he struggles to engage his lower half to take full advantage of his 6-foot-3 frame. An above-average 85-86 mph slider with hard, late break shows flashes of a true swing-and-miss pitch. Riley's other breaking pitch is an 11-5 power curveball that sits 77-80 mph featuring late bite. This pitch also has plus whiff potential. He also offers a mid-80s average changeup. Riley's ceiling will depend on how he develops his fastball command and employs his lower half more efficiently. With two potential plus offspeed pitches, he certainly has a solid base to build on.

Personal Cheeseball

PC Trey Harris   OF
Born: 01/15/96   Age: 24   Bats: R   Throws: R   Height: 5'8"   Weight: 215
Origin: Round 32, 2018 Draft (#952 overall)

One of the most fun things in what we do is to watch the development of a player like Harris. He got a $10,000 bonus as a senior sign 32nd-round pick out of the University of Missouri in the 2018 draft, but he quickly rose above the expectations that might have come with that background. When I went to see the Mississippi Braves play this season, I was interested to see all of the big name prospects on that roster, but the guy who stood out most to me was Harris.

He has a compact, athletic build at 5-foot-10 and 215 pounds and a collection of mostly average-to-a-tick-above tools. What he does is put all of those tools together in a way that makes him at least a bit intriguing. Harris is balanced at the plate with good timing, though he is a free-swinger and he seems to be focused on making contact to the middle of the field. In 14 at-bats, he put the ball in play 13 times, with all of them going from right-center to left-center. It wasn't just defensive contact, either, as he hit three balls to deep left-center, including one of only two balls I've seen go out to that part of the park in Jacksonville in four seasons of watching games there.

Defensively, Harris' arm is just average, but it seemed at least adequate for right field and he did take good routes to fly balls. He needs to figure out how to combine his aggressiveness with just a bit more selectivity to help him improve his walk rates and give him a better opportunity to recognize when he can turn on pitches and do more damage to the pull side. If he can find that happy medium, he has a floor of a short-side platoon player and if it all comes together, he could find regular at-bats. That's a nice outcome for a 32nd-round pick.

Low Minors Sleeper

LMS

Vaughn Grissom   SS
Born: 01/05/01   Age: 19   Bats: R   Throws: R   Height: 6'3"   Weight: 180
Origin: Round 11, 2019 Draft (#337 overall)

There were a few options for Atlanta's low minors sleeper pick this year, because the organization drafted several projectable prep athletes after the 10th round this past June in an effort to shore up lower-level depth. A year from now we may be discussing names like Tyler Owens and Jared Johnson as the next system risers, but Grissom gets the nod right now for his exciting potential with the bat. He earned one of the highest signing bonuses of the 11th round for his highly-projectable frame and potential to be a corner masher. He'll likely move off shortstop as he grows and they'll need to evaluate his arm strength going forward for a potential fit at third, but second base or the outfield could also be possibilities down the road. Grissom's bat is the big draw, showing a feel to hit with a loose, quick stroke and present strength when he catches one out front. As he grows, he could develop impact power along with solid barrel awareness and plate discipline. His eventual defensive home is a bit up in the air, but it's easy to get excited about the bat as he develops.

Top Talents 25 and Under (as of 4/1/2020)

1. Ronald Acuña Jr.

2. Mike Soroka
3. Ozzie Albies
4. Cristian Pache
5. Ian Anderson
6. Drew Waters
7. Austin Riley
8. Kyle Muller
9. Shea Langeliers
10. Kyle Wright

You know things are going well for you when you produce the runner-up in NL Rookie of the Year voting the year after you produce the actual winner of the thing. That's where the Braves are when it comes to their young talent, and it's absolutely conceivable that another wave is on the way to complement the wave that has already hit Atlanta and is thriving as well.

Both Ronald Acuña and Mike Soroka are going to be on top of this list for a while. Soroka is coming off of a rookie season where he eventually established himself at the top of the rotation and should be there for years to come. Then there's Acuña, who squashed any rumors of a "sophomore slump" by making a serious run at a 40/40 season. Both of those players were in their age-21 season, which means that they've still got plenty of potential left to realize.

Ozzie Albies may be a couple of years older, but he's still just as dynamic as the two aforementioned players. The most pleasant surprise about Ozzie has been his bat, as he's hit 48 home runs over the past couple of seasons. This was after he earned a reputation as a light-hitting, defense-first infielder during his time on the farm. Now he's got the bat and the defense is just as good, so he is absolutely in a good place right now.

While Austin Riley came onto the major-league scene like a lion, he eventually calmed down and was forced to transform into a lamb once the pitchers caught up to his approach on the plate. The flashes of potential he showed during his early days as a major leaguer were brilliant and if he can come anywhere close to that on a consistent basis, then he could go up in this ranking as he gets closer to reaching the age limit here.

However, the next wave of talent that is still plying their craft in Atlanta's farm system is worth dreaming about if you're a Braves fan. Cristian Pache has truly come into his own as a professional and it seems inevitable that the defensive dynamo will be joining Acuña in the outfield at some point in 2020. The same could be said for Drew Waters, who had a wonderful season in the minors and is also primed to make an arrival in the upcoming season. If those two live up to the lofty level of play that Acuña has set, then Atlanta's outfield could be set in stone for a long time.

Then there's the pitching. During the initial stages of their relatively quick rebuild, the Braves loaded up on pitching prospects and that was initially the star of this farm system's story. As the position players developed, the pitching prospects seemed to fall off. However, there's still good stuff to be excited about, as Kyle Wright and Kyle Muller are still projected to be solid arms and Ian Anderson continues to stand tall (both literally and figuratively) as the top hurler in the farm system.

While Atlanta's minor league strength may not be as formidable as it once was, it also comes with the understandable caveat that a lot of the stars of this system are graduating to become stars at the big league level. The first big wave of young talent has already shown its stuff at the top level, and we're getting closer to the day when the second big wave gets its chance as well.

Part 3: Featured Articles

The Baseball Is Juiced (Again)

Robert Arthur

This article originally appeared at Baseball Prospectus on April 5, 2019.

It started when the normally reliable Chris Sale got lit up for three homers by the Mariners in the Red Sox's season opener. It was part of a record number of taters that flew on Opening Day, as starters from Sale to Zack Greinke were taken deep by the handful. Then Christian Yelich hit a home run in each of his first four games, tying yet another MLB record, this one for consecutive games with a dinger to start a season.

It didn't take long for fans and players to begin whispering and tweeting about the baseballs being juiced again. It's early yet for us to come to any definitive conclusion about the 2019 season, but preliminary data shows that the baseball has returned to its aerodynamic peak. Whether that means this season will smash home run records like 2017 did remains to be seen.

Before home run explosion over the last few years, no one worried too much about the baseball's air resistance. While MLB and Rawlings (the company that manufactures the official baseballs) kept track of dozens of metrics to make sure that the ball was consistent from month to month, they didn't measure drag.

But drag is incredibly important in determining how likely a hitter is to knock one out of the park. As baseballs become more aerodynamic, they travel further given a certain initial velocity. A deep fly ball that might have been caught at the warning track can instead go into the first row of the stands. A three percent change in drag coefficient can work to add about five feet to a well-hit fly ball, which can in turn increase home runs league wide by an astounding 10-15 percent.

It's possible to measure the aerodynamics of the baseball using the pitch-tracking radars currently in place in each MLB ballpark. By calculating the loss of speed from when the pitch is released to when it crosses the plate, you can directly measure the drag coefficient on the baseball. I first wrote about the role of decreasing drag in boosting home runs in 2017, and MLB's commission of scientists and statisticians later confirmed that the more aerodynamic baseballs in use that year were largely to blame for the spike in home runs. The same commission rejected some alternate hypotheses, like rising temperatures and a league-wide boost in launch angle pushing more balls over the fence.

The current era has featured some large fluctuations in drag coefficient, leading to first an explosion in 2016 and 2017, and then a dialing back of homers last year. Curious about the record-breaking home run tallies in the last few days, I used the same methodology to measure the aerodynamics of the baseballs so far in 2019.

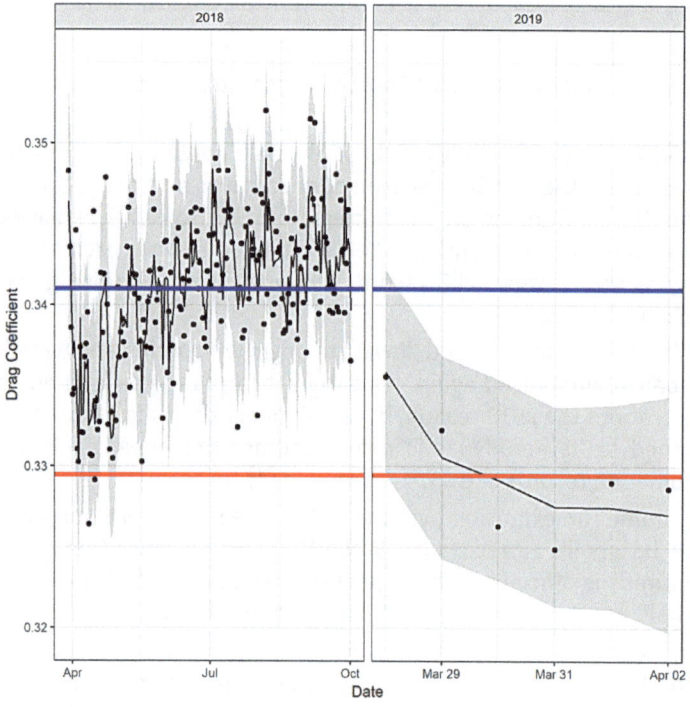

We're only a week into the 2019 season, but the drag numbers so far are among the lowest recorded in the last calendar year. With apologies for gory math, the current 2019 season average drag coefficient (the red line) would be below the 95 percent credible interval (the shaded area) for about nine-tenths of the 2018 season. (I used a Bayesian Random Walk model implemented in INLA to calculate these credible intervals, averaging the drag numbers in each game and adjusting for park.)

There were only a handful of six-day stretches in 2018 that had drag numbers below what we're seeing now, and most were in late June and early July. All of this means that 2019's data so far is quite a bit different than what we saw through most of last year.

These drag coefficients factor out the effects of temperature and air density, so they aren't a product of April cold. However, the numbers could be deceptive if the radars used to track pitches have changed from year to year. I consulted with some experts within baseball who were not aware of any specific modifications to the radar this year that could produce this pattern, but it's an important caveat of which to be aware.

On the one hand, it's only been six days, and we don't quite have the statistical basis to say that these drag coefficients are unprecedented compared to 2018. On the other hand, we've witnessed about 5,000 fastballs so far this season, so it's not as if our sample size is small. At least so far, the baseball has played like it's much more aerodynamic than it was last year. In fact, the current drag coefficient is really only comparable to 2017, when the baseballs were more aerodynamic than they had been in at least a decade.

It's not just fancy radar tracking indicating that the baseball is flying through the air more easily. The current number of home runs per game (as of this writing) is the highest it's been since the heady days of 2017, the year that teams and players broke dinger-related records everywhere you looked. That's especially remarkable considering that we're in what is typically the coldest part of the regular season, when lower temperatures and higher winds tend to suppress offense and keep balls in the air within the park. Comparing only from April to April, this year's rate of home runs per fly ball is even a little bit higher than it was in 2017.

With that said, the current measurements are no guarantee that 2019 will be another year of record-shattering homer hitting. The trouble with the drag measurements is that they are not consistent from June to August, from week to week, or even sometimes from day to day. Whether because of natural manufacturing variation or differences in the underlying supplies of cowhide and thread that go into the baseballs, drag has a tendency to fluctuate up and down over the course of a year. So the homers that fly in the first week of April wouldn't necessarily clear the fence a week later.

It's possible that this one-week drop in drag coefficient subsides and the baseball returns to its 2018 levels. On the other hand, it's almost equally probable that the ball becomes even more slippery and flies ever farther. Either way, it's clear that the baseball's air resistance is something to keep an eye on for the remainder of the 2019 season.

—*Robert Arthur is an author of Baseball Prospectus.*

The Moral Hazard of Playing It Safe

Craig Goldstein

This article originally appeared at Baseball Prospectus on August 6, 2019.

A couple days prior to the trade deadline, amidst a sea of tranquility posing as the lead up to the trade deadline, Bob Nightengale took to Twitter. Nightengale, who was probably wearing his pants backwards at the time, tweeted that MLB GMs were coming around on the idea that the unified trade deadline should be moved back from July 31 to August 15, so they could better assess their positions in the standings and whether they should buy or sell. To which I said:

This might strike some as reductive and churlish. And it might be that, but it isn't really wrong, either. Jeff Quinton wrote a great piece discussing the environmental factors that enable front offices to avoid risk without upsetting the apple cart within their own fanbases. I don't believe that it goes far enough, however. His article gives us the proper framework through which to understand why these behaviors have been allowed to seep into front offices throughout the league. Understanding the reasons behind these actions are different from excusing them, though, and GMs should not be let off the hook for their non-competitive approach to the trade deadline (much less the offseason).

⚾   ⚾   ⚾

It's fair to say that fans as a group have rarely, if ever, been pro-player. It is also fair to say that in the time during and following the Moneyball revolution, the pendulum swung from fans who cared intensely about winning in the moment (and thus might be intolerant of a rebuilding approach) to fans who supported building a team that could compete throughout multiple seasons, viewing the playoffs as a crapshoot, with the thought that getting multiple bites at the apple was a better approach than taking a bigger bite in any one season.

There's nothing wrong with that approach, and I still find merit in that argument. However, it seems that the pendulum has swung too far in that direction. Teams are overvaluing some of the individual factors that make themselves long-term contenders rather than attempting to seize a championship when given the opportunity. It's a difficult needle to thread.

And surely, they (and those in similar positions) would have liked another two weeks to clarify where they stand so as to better marshal their resources. We've all asked for a few more minutes when staring at a menu. But all of these GMs and front office personnel are where they are to make difficult decisions. They have proprietary data and internal analysts dedicated to understanding their position relative to the rest of the league, and how any move in the here and now impacts their long-term vision. To complain (if that report is accurate) that over half the season is not enough to properly assess their season is bullshit of the highest order. Move the deadline, and you'd simply have increasingly discounted trade offers because teams would be acquiring even less control of anyone they're acquiring, rental or not.

Major league front offices are behaving like the managers they lampooned two decades ago. They're effectively sacrificing a runner to second in the ninth inning—not because it's the correct move, but rather because it is safe. It used to be that the phrase "moral hazard" was used to describe general managers who made ill-fated, short-sighted decisions aimed at locking in wins and securing their jobs at the expense of their team's future. Now, general managers are guilty of committing moral hazards in the opposite direction, playing it utterly safe and terrified of becoming scapegoats.

In lieu of bold action, they opt to pussyfoot around a current window of contention, choosing instead to play the long game and stack up years of control like they're blocks in a game of Jenga. GMs pass on signing quality players in free agency because the back-end of the deal might look bad, and because they might be able to squeeze out 70 percent of the production from a player who costs a tenth as much. That's a safer investment, too, because it's also hard to prove a negative—it's impossible to prove that Manny Machado would make the Mets a playoff team in 2019-2020, but it's easy to say that the back half of Robinson Cano's contract sucks. Owners, who rule over GM's jobs, are also humans with human brain processes that will always make the so-called albatross contract uglier than the road not taken.

These days, GMs are remembered for the bad deals they make and the surplus value they generate, not the acquisition of expensive, necessary talents that meet their market worth (or fall slightly short while still providing significant on-field value). And front offices know that one or two expensive misfires can cost them their jobs, no matter how many good deals they make.

No front office exemplifies this ethos more than the Toronto Blue Jays. General Manager Ross Atkins had this to say following the Blue Jays underwhelming trade deadline:

This is by no means the first time that an executive will cite years of control to justify their actions, which is often just another way of saying "don't look at what we got, look at how much we got of it." Atkins touts quantity to elide the discussion of quality—either, that of the players acquired, or those given up. Remember: the other teams presumably value years of control, too.

Atkins also had some thoughts to offer regarding free agents back in early 2018:

Atlanta Braves 2020

This ignores, of course, whether the player can create enough value in the front end of a contract to justify the longer term of a deal, and the decline that often occurs in the back end. It also ignores whether the player can fill a need the team requires and put them in a position to compete for and win a championship. But as teams seemingly avoid contention at all, where they might end up having to consider and later justify some of these tough decisions, we still see risk-averse approaches.

Anthony Fenech's article on two trades that recently extended GM Al Avila didn't make got at this issue rather well:

> Passing on those deals was defensible: Both players had yet to break out and trading [Michael] Fulmer—a pitcher who appeared to be a future ace, no matter his injury concerns—would have taken serious gumption, opening Avila up to strong criticism.

Avoiding strong criticism is something each of us can understand as a motivation, but the avoidance of criticism only matters if that criticism is valid. In Fulmer's case, shoving his injury concerns aside affects not only the years that the team controls him (he is currently missing a full season due to Tommy John surgery) but also the quality of those seasons, as his knee and elbow injuries combined to dampen his effectiveness even when healthy enough to pitch. But it was easy to present the then-current image of Fulmer as a top of the rotation pitcher who the team had under its domain for the next five seasons as something to build around. The status quo isn't nearly as often second-guessed as a decision that disrupts it.

⚾ ⚾ ⚾

MLB GMs are risk-averse to a fault. They are ivy-educated and consulting firm-approved, and yet they can't seem to avoid leaving wins on the table in their all-consuming lust for a non-existent $/WAR championship. They are supposed to zig when everyone else zags, and not merely pay lip service to the idea of zigging through a calculated PR plan built on convincing the fan base their approach is novel when it actually apes most of their competitors. Instead they've become far more concerned with making safe, accepted-by-the-new-common-wisdom decisions, such that our prior understanding of what a moral hazard is has become inverted.

I can't blame them entirely, and not only because of the reasons that Quinton illuminated in his article, but also because of the damage wrought by the introduction of the second wild card (WC2) spot. MLB's desire to have more teams in playoff contention has sparked anti-competitive behavior. Teams know now that they do not need to swing big as they assemble their roster because there is a good chance that a mediocre team can either catch fire and capture a division, or muddle along until they back into the WC2.

Simultaneously, the one-game playoff has neutered the WC1, putting an entire season on the flip of a coin like some sort of baseball-obsessed Anton Chigurh. While the one-game playoff makes sense as a way to increase the value of winning a division, it also means that if a front office doesn't like its chances of overcoming a behemoth like the Dodgers or Astros in the offseason, they have few incentives to chase glory. Similarly, the relative inaction in the NL Central at the trade deadline—despite a wide open division—can be explained by the idea that any high-variance investment could still result in only a wild card (or worse) result, given the mere two months left in the season to make an impact.

⚾   ⚾   ⚾

As stated at the top, we should not confuse reasons for excuses. The implementation of the second wild card is just one of many environmental factors that influence how each front office operates. I am convinced that it is one of the larger factors, but I am also convinced that organizations need to shed the yoke of "efficiency at all costs" so that they can instead pursue competition, as the spirit of the game intends. Until they do, we're all deadline losers.

—*Craig Goldstein is an author of Baseball Prospectus.*

Index of Names

Acuña Jr., Ronald 81
Albies, Ozzie 18
Alexander, CJ 94
Anderson, Ian 89, 100
Backstrom, Mahki 94
Ball, Bryce 94, 107
Blevins, Jerry 96
Burrows, Thomas 96
Camargo, Johan 20
Contreras, William 82, 104
Culberson, Charlie 22
d'Arnaud, Travis 44
Davidson, Tucker 96, 110
Dayton, Grant 96
De La Cruz, Jasseel 96, 106
Dean, Justin 94
Duda, Lucas 94
Duvall, Adam 24
Flowers, Tyler 26
Foltynewicz, Mike 46
Freeman, Freddie 28
Fried, Max 48
Greene, Shane 50
Grissom, Vaughn 112
Hamels, Cole 52
Harris, Michael 83, 109
Harris, Trey 94, 111
Hechavarría, Adeiny 30
Hernandez, Daysbel 96
Hernández, Félix 54
Higginbotham, Jake 96
Inciarte, Ender 32
Jackson, Alex 94, 108
Jackson, Luke 57
Jenista, Greyson 84, 110
Langeliers, Shea 85, 102
Markakis, Nick 34
Martin, Chris 59
McCann, Brian 36
Melancon, Mark 61
Minter, A.J. 63
Muller, Kyle 90, 101
Murphy, John Ryan 94
Newcomb, Sean 65
O'Day, Darren 91
Ortega, Rafael 94
Ozuna, Marcell 38
Pache, Cristian 86, 99
Pfeifer, Philip 96
Philip, Beau 94
Ramos, Jefrey 94
Riley, Austin 40
Riley, Trey 96, 111
Shewmake, Braden 87, 105
Smith, Will 67
Sobotka, Chad 96
Soroka, Mike 69
Swanson, Dansby 42
Tarnok, Freddy 96, 107
Tomlin, Josh 71
Toussaint, Touki 73
Vodnik, Victor 92, 109

Walker, Jeremy 96	Wilson, Bryse 77, 104
Waters, Drew 88, 101	Wright, Kyle 79, 103
Webb, Jacob 75	Ynoa, Huascar 96, 108
Weigel, Patrick 93, 110	